I0199923

# INSTANT TEAM BUILDING

## Other Books in the Instant Success Series

*Successful Franchising* by Bradley J. Sugars
*The Real Estate Coach* by Bradley J. Sugars
*Billionaire in Training* by Bradley J. Sugars
*Instant Cashflow* by Bradley J. Sugars
*Instant Sales* by Bradley J. Sugars
*Instant Leads* by Bradley J. Sugars
*Instant Profit* by Bradley J. Sugars
*Instant Promotions* by Bradley J. Sugars
*Instant Repeat Business* by Bradley J. Sugars
*The Business Coach* by Bradley J. Sugars
*Instant Systems* by Bradley J. Sugars
*Instant Referrals* by Bradley J. Sugars
*Instant Advertising* by Bradley J. Sugars

# INSTANT TEAM BUILDING

BRADLEY J. SUGARS

**McGraw-Hill**
New York Chicago San Francisco Lisbon London
Madrid Mexico City Milan New Delhi San Juan
Seoul Singapore Sydney Toronto

The McGraw-Hill Companies



1 2 3 4 5 6 7 8 9 0 FGR/FGR 0 9 8 7 6 5

ISBN 978-0-07-183161-1

This publication is designed to provide accurate and authoritative information in regard to the subject matter covered. It is sold with the understanding that neither the author nor the publisher is engaged in rendering legal, accounting, or other professional service. If legal advice or other expert assistance is required, the services of a competent professional person should be sought.
—From a Declaration of Principles jointly adopted by Committee of the American Bar Association and a Committee of Publishers.

McGraw-Hill books are available at special quantity discounts to use as premiums and sales promotions, or for use in corporate training programs. For more information, please write to the Director of Special Sales, McGraw-Hill Professional, Two Penn Plaza, New York, NY 10121-2298. Or contact your local bookstore.

Library of Congess Cataloging-in-Publication Data
Sugars, Bradley J.
Instant team building / Bradley J. Sugars.
p. cm.

1. Teams in the workplace. I. Title.
HD66.S837 2006
658.4'022—dc22 2005025346

The important thing to recognize is that it takes a team, and the team ought to get credit for the wins and the losses. Successes have many fathers; failures have none.

**Philip Caldwell**

# CONTENTS


Introduction . . . . . . . . . . . . . . . . . . . . . . . . . . . . . . . . . . . . . . . . . . .ix

About This Book . . . . . . . . . . . . . . . . . . . . . . . . . . . . . . . . . . . . . . . .xi

Charlie Builds His Dream Team . . . . . . . . . . . . . . . . . . . . . . . . . . . . .xiii

PART 1—Vision, Mission, and Culture . . . . . . . . . . . . . . . . . . . . . . . . .1

PART 2—Putting Together the Dream Team . . . . . . . . . . . . . . . . . . . . . .11

PART 3—Six Keys to a Winning Team . . . . . . . . . . . . . . . . . . . . . . . . .29

PART 4—Getting the Environment Right . . . . . . . . . . . . . . . . . . . . . .41

PART 5—Put Systems in Place . . . . . . . . . . . . . . . . . . . . . . . . . . . . . .49

PART 6—Recruiting Team Members . . . . . . . . . . . . . . . . . . . . . . . . . .57

PART 7—Getting the Beliefs Right . . . . . . . . . . . . . . . . . . . . . . . . . .81

PART 8—Synergy . . . . . . . . . . . . . . . . . . . . . . . . . . . . . . . . . . . . . . .105

Conclusion . . . . . . . . . . . . . . . . . . . . . . . . . . . . . . . . . . . . . . . . . .119

Getting into *Action* . . . . . . . . . . . . . . . . . . . . . . . . . . . . . . . . . . . .121

About the Author . . . . . . . . . . . . . . . . . . . . . . . . . . . . . . . . . . . . 125

Recommended Reading List . . . . . . . . . . . . . . . . . . . . . . . . . . . . . . 127

The 18 Most Asked Questions about Working with an **ActionCOACH** Business Coach . . . . . . . . . . . . . . . . . . . . . . . . . . . . . . 129

**ActionCOACH** Contact Details . . . . . . . . . . . . . . . . . . . . . . . . . . . . . . 141

# INTRODUCTION

I'm sure you've heard the old cliché "people are a company's best asset." In many ways it's true.

You've probably also heard the cliché "a chain is only as strong as its weakest link." Again, a very true saying.

But there's another truism that you might not have heard. It's something my Dad told me many years ago when I was struggling to find what I believed to be decent people with whom to staff my fledgling company. I still remember the words as clear as if he were saying them today. "You only ever get the staff you deserve." It was on that day when my Dad helped me realize everything that goes on in my business is a reflection of either my ability or my inability.

It still amazes me to this day how a business is a reflection of its owner. Some owners want to control everything and wonder why their team never wants to take the initiative. Some hate selling and love paperwork, so they've always got their numbers done, but never really seem to sell too much, and so on. It almost feels like your business is designed to teach you everything you don't know.

And, as my Dad pointed out, the people you attract in your life are another great mirror of where you are in your life. It wasn't until I became a great person, a great businessman, and a great leader, that I started to attract great people. And *attract* great people I did.

When you reach this level it's rarely necessary to go looking for people; they usually come to you.

The poor quality of staff seems to be a perennial topic among business owners, but is this a true reflection of the state of the labor market? Or is there something more fundamentally wrong with the general situation? How can it be that out of all the thousands of people looking for jobs at any point in time, business owners can't find decent candidates from which to choose?

Perhaps the problem lies with the business owners and not the candidates. Perhaps business owners are going about finding and selecting candidates in the wrong manner. Perhaps they are basing their selections on false criteria.

But is there more to selecting a dream team than this? Does luck play a role, as some suggest? What about the business itself? Do good businesses *attract* good people, while average businesses *attract* average people? Or is it the other way around?

If all of this rings a bell, then read on. This book is designed to give you the inside track on everything you need to know about how to put together that dream team you've always wanted. It aims at providing you with an *instant* guide on how to go about making sure the people you select are just perfect for your business. Once you've read the book, you'll know precisely what it takes to ensure that you have round pegs in round holes, and not square pegs in round holes, as so often is the case.

So congratulations on deciding to take proactive steps to develop your business. This book is the next step in your company's success story. From this moment on, you won't have to dream about the day when you're recognized as a leader in your field. You'll know precisely what to do to make it a reality. You'll also know exactly how to go about ensuring your business employs only the very best people—people who are a perfect fit for your business and the rest of your team.

# ABOUT THIS BOOK

This book is divided into different parts, one for each of the major factors that contribute towards finding, and keeping, your dream team.

You can work through this book from beginning to end to gain an inside track on how to find dream candidates for your business, even better than professional recruitment agencies would, or you can simply pick the one that interests you most, jump straight in and begin working through the steps outlined. Either way, you'll discover just how easy it is to take your business to new levels of efficiency, fun, and profitability.

Each easy-to-understand stage covers an important aspect of the whole business of building a winning team. You see, there are things you must give careful consideration to before jumping in and hiring people on the strength of their resumes and a superficial interview.

You might decide to implement all the great ideas explained in this book all at once, or you might decide to implement them one at a time. But whatever you decide, the important thing is that you'll no longer be blundering around in the dark, unsure whether what you're doing has a chance of helping you to achieve one of business' most elusive goals—the establishment of a dream team.

We'll start by visiting Charlie, my trusted mechanic, who was having trouble finding good mechanics to employ, and even more trouble hanging on to them when he did. His case is typical. See what he did to resolve these challenges.

Then read through each remaining chapter of the book and discover things you might never have known about this dynamic and vitally important subject. You might also be surprised at how much this exercise will reveal about your business. It may get you thinking about important issues you've never thought about before. If some of this information is new to you, don't be concerned—there's never been a better time to start than *now.*

Now it's time to get started. It's time to get into *Action.*

# CHARLIE BUILDS HIS DREAM TEAM

I knew Charlie was struggling when it came to the subject of staff. I had noticed a few new faces in the workshop every time I visited. It was almost like he was involved in training new apprentices; they came and went with such frequency.

He assured me this was normal in the industry. I knew otherwise. Or at least I knew no one needed to put up with this state of affairs if he didn't want to. But the truth of the matter was that most accepted it because they simply didn't know otherwise. And Charlie was no different.

I told him as much during a recent visit, and he appeared dumbstruck. "I know I shouldn't be surprised, Brad, because everything you've taught me so far should tell me that you always take a different approach to business, but still, I just can't imagine how it would be possible to operate otherwise in the automobile industry."

I smiled and offered to explain all at a future date, if that's what he would like.

He agreed, and I set a date in my appointment book.

So it was with more than a little excitement that I pulled up outside his garage and headed for his office. I knew this was going to be an amazing session, because I really love teaching people how to go about putting a dream team together. You see, the basics are really nothing more than common sense, yet somehow common sense seems to have been forgotten over the years. Dealing with people is, after all, what business is really all about, isn't it? Yet how few business people recognize this.

"Hi, Charlie. Nice seeing you again," I said as he stood to greet me as I entered his cluttered office.

"Hi, Brad. As always, it's a pleasure having you here. Come on in and grab yourself a seat."

"Busy day today, Charlie?" I asked. I already knew the answer, because he usually waited outside his garage for me to arrive, but this time he hadn't. That struck me as unusual because he always loved seeing which car I would roll up in.

"Yes, you won't believe it, but this morning one of my mechanics phoned in to say he won't be coming back. Received a fantastic offer from one of the main dealerships in town. It's funny, isn't it, happening on the very day we're getting together to talk about team building."

I smiled and immediately thought about how our brain's Reticular Activating System works.

"You want to know something, Charlie?" I responded. "I don't find that unusual at all, knowing what I do about our Reticular Activating Systems. Remember, we spoke about this before."

"Yes I do, Brad, but can you run it past me one more time? You know what I'm like, man."

"Sure. It all began in 1949 when two neuroscientists by the name of Magoun and Moruzzi discovered that we have a thing called the Reticular Activating System in our brains."

I thought he would remember this best if I explained, in story form, how it was discovered and what the implications of the discovery were for us as business people.

"They found that if a portion of the very core of an animal's brain stem were to be stimulated, an immediate arousal of the cortex resulted, with the animal becoming alert and oriented to its environment. If the animal were sleepy, it would immediately become alert. What they further discovered was that this area of the brain was the beginning of an extended system that focuses on various aspects of consciousness. They found that this process could actually be controlled by the various processes of the brain to ensure only that which is most relevant at the time is focused upon. Are you with me?"

"Yes, Brad, go on."

"It's this that interests me most. You see, a good example of this is the pricking up of the hairs on the back of our necks when we sense someone standing or creeping up behind us on a dark night. It allows us to immediately become aware of something that we didn't even know was there at the time. Similarly, if you had to concentrate on playing a difficult piece of music, your brain would be able to shut out those distracting sounds from the audience that would normally force you into making a mistake."

"Very interesting, I'm sure, but what has it to do with my mechanics?"

I could tell he was becoming confused, yet he was still listening intently. This was what I wanted, as he was going to have to do a whole lot of listening that day.

"You'll see soon enough, Charlie. I know from my research and experience that we can control our ideas, which in turn can affect or control our existence."

He was beginning to look puzzled.

"Let me explain. Remember back to the last time you bought a car. All of a sudden you noticed that there were hundreds of them on the road. Your Reticular Activating System will find proof that good mechanics are hard to come by and keep, if that's what you believe."

"Ah, I'm beginning to see where you're coming from, Brad."

Time for another example that he would be able to relate to.

"Remember when you were a kid and your mother sent you to the shop, saying, '*Don't forget* to buy some milk.' What did you do? You forgot the milk."

A smile shot across his face. I knew he would relate to this.

"Yeah, Brad, why was that?"

"It has to do with the fact that your brain doesn't work on negatives. It didn't flag the word 'don't' in its memory banks for action. What it did spotlight was the words 'forget' and 'milk.' It kept highlighting 'forget' and 'milk' while you walked to the shop and while you wandered up and down the aisles wondering what it was you had to buy."

"It's just like the last time you said to yourself, 'Don't forget, don't forget, don't forget.' What happened? You forgot. What you should have done instead was to change your wording to 'remember'. Be positive. Your mother should have said: 'Remember the milk.' "

Charlie was actually laughing quietly to himself as I spoke. But I didn't mind because I could tell that he actually understood what I was telling him. He *really* understood, and he could personalize my message. He could actually relate to it.

"Remember to ask for the things you want, *not* to push away what you don't want, Charlie. Every day your business meets your true expectations. In other words, if you believe you've got to work hard to make money, then that will always be your reality. If you believe you can never get good people to work for you, that'll be your reality. Remember too that you generally make true what you believe to be so. We even have a term for this because it's so well accepted. It's called a self-fulfilling prophecy. Isn't that interesting?"

"You're right, Brad. As usual, what you're telling me is fascinating. Keep going."

"What I want you to be aware of at this stage is that there is a thing called a Reticular Activating System in your brain, and it's something very powerful that you can use to make your dreams come true. And that's why the fact that you have a fairly high turnover rate with your mechanics doesn't surprise me at all. It's simply because that's what you expect it to be, Charlie. But it doesn't have to be that way. In a moment we're going to discuss why."

Charlie leaned back in his chair, took in a deep breath, and then breathed out loudly.

"I'm so glad it doesn't have to be like this, Brad. I can't wait to find out what I can do about it."

"There's so much more to hiring the right people. Charlie. You know, most companies go about this entirely wrongly, in my view. They access their candidates against the wrong set of criteria. And as for their selection processes—well, suffice to say at this stage that I go about it the other way around. You see, I hold a deselection process at my company and it gives me great results every time. I go about finding and selecting my team members in the opposite way to what most businesses do."

I could tell that he was intrigued and desperate to find out more.

"As usual, Charlie, I'll run through things from the beginning, so you get a good understanding of everything you'll need to put together your dream team. How does that sound?"

"Fantastic. Want a drink now, or should we dive straight in?"

"Let's move on. I can tell you want to."

# INSTANT TEAM BUILDING

# Part 1

## Vision, Mission, and Culture

The first place to look when setting out to assemble your dream team is at your company. Remember what I said about only getting the staff you deserve? If you want to attract a better quality of person than the ones you currently employ, then you've got to change various things about your company.

It's just like baking a cake. If you've always baked chocolate cakes, but now you want to try an apple crumble, then it's no use sticking with the recipe for the chocolate cake. You've got to get a recipe for an apple crumble. If you don't, you'll continue to produce chocolate cakes. It's as simple as that.

So how do you go about changing your company to attract the type of person you're after? You need to go back to basics and review your vision, mission, and culture.

Yes, that's right. You need to re-examine the very fundamentals of your business. You need to look at its core values and ideals and then change or realign those that would deter would-be team members.

So how do you do that?

Well, start with your company's vision. By the way, it may surprise you to know that the vast majority of businesses don't actually have a Vision Statement. Yes, I know the owner may have a rough idea of where the company is going or where it would be nice for it to go, but the point is most don't have a well-thought-out and articulated Vision Statement that is written down for all to see.

And here's something else that may surprise you: Of those companies that do have a Vision Statement, the vast majority seem intent on keeping it a secret. That's right. No one except a handful of their senior executives know anything about it at all. I often ask the first person I come across when visiting a business—usually the receptionist—what the company's vision is, and do you know what?

They never can tell me. I find this shocking, because if a company's people don't know what they are aiming for, how will they know in which direction to aim? How will they know what their progress is and whether they are moving closer to or further away from achieving that vision?

I'm a firm believer in giving people ownership of the overall vision of a business; in that way they will all strive for the same thing. They will also all have similar values and appreciate the same general ideals. They will all identify with the business and with each other as team members.

So, what then should a company's Vision Statement contain? What, for that matter, is a Vision Statement?

Let me answer that by means of an example. I'll use one of my companies, **ActionCOACH,** as an example.

When I set out to build this company, I built it with the end in mind. In other words, I built it according to how I envisaged it when it was finished. This is very important, because it affects everything you do in your building stage. Your vision, mission, and goals will have to take this into account.

My vision for **ActionCOACH** is:

World Abundance through Business Reeducation

Notice it is *world* abundance, not *Australian* or *Southeast Queensland* abundance. This sets the tone for the whole company and its future. It also dictates how others see us.

The Vision Statement is the long-term goal of your business. And by long-term, I mean 100 years. Don't mess around with short-term goals here. We're talking about the grand picture of what your business will be like when its finished. Think of it as the strategic intent of the business.

Vision Statements are meant to be living documents. By that I mean they mustn't just hang in the boardroom or some other hallowed place where they never get seen. They should be prominently displayed all over the place where absolutely everyone can see them all the time. You see, it's critical that your entire team identifies with the Vision Statement and accepts it as the team's vision too.

Whenever I recruit new team members, the very first thing I discuss with them is our vision. I let them know what we are striving for. If they can't identify with it, I tell them they're welcome to leave then and there.

Let's now consider the Mission Statement.

Again, many businesses simply don't have one. If yours is one of them, then before you do anything else, spend some time developing one. But before you do, do you know what a Mission Statement is?

The Mission Statement states how your business is going to accomplish its vision. It is obviously going to be very much more detailed than the Vision Statement. It should clearly spell out the following:

- Who you are.
- What business you are in.
- Who your customers are.
- What makes you different from your competition.

This last point is very important. It's something you need to spend time getting clear in your own mind first. You see, the day you differentiate yourself from the rest, you won't have to compete on price anymore. That's why a Giorgio Armani shirt costs very much more than one from K-Mart. I mean, they might very well be made from the same material and in the same factory, but the Giorgio Armani costs more precisely because of marketing differentiation.

To illustrate what I'm getting at, let's consider the Mission Statement of my company, **ActionCOACH.**

> **ActionCOACH** is a team of committed, positive and successful people who are always striving to be balanced, integrated, and honest. We will work within our *14 Points of Culture* to make sure that everyone who touches or is touched by the **ActionCOACH** team members will benefit greatly and in some way move closer to becoming the people they want to be or achieve the goals they want to achieve.

We will always work in "co-opetition" with all those who believe they are in competition with us.

We are in the business of "Edutainment." We will educate ourselves, our clients, and all those whom we work with, while we entertain them and create a fun learning environment. We will educate our clients in world-class marketing and business development techniques using audio, video, CDs, other technologies, and simple workbooks, workshops, and seminar formats.

Our products and services will be of the highest quality, value for money, and, whether sourced from within the company or externally will always add the most value and use the latest and most effective training methodologies available.

**ActionCOACH** clients whether they be small, medium, or large in size will have a desire to have us help them in achieving their goals and be able to take on our commitment to them by returning their Commitment to **ActionCOACH.** They will be forward thinking, willing to learn and grow, and be willing to work as team players in the development of an organization of "people."

Our clients will be selected more on attitude than size, and they will want to deal with us because we understand people are important, systems should run a company, we offer the most practical, most applicable, and fastest strategies of growth, and most importantly because we mean what we say.

We will give people back their spirit and freedom through business development.

Once again, this is discussed with every applicant during the interview process. It is explained and talked about at length. Applicants are given the opportunity to ask questions and to say if they feel comfortable or uncomfortable with it. If they don't agree with it or feel it doesn't excite them, they are invited to leave and look for a company that better matches their outlook.

Here are a few great questions to ask yourself when developing your Mission Statement:

1. What do you, as a team, want more of?
2. What do you, as a team, want less of?
3. Describe the kinds of relationships you wish to have with your

   - Customers
   - Suppliers
   - Shareholders
   - Competitors
   - Community
   - Employees

Once you have written down your Mission Statement, look over the statements below and check those that are true:

___ Is the Mission Statement future oriented?

___ Is the Mission Statement likely to lead to a better future for the organization?

___ Is the Mission Statement consistent with the organization's values?

___ Does the Mission Statement set standards of excellence?

___ Does the Mission Statement clarify purpose and direction?

___ Does the Mission Statement inspire enthusiasm and encourage commitment?

___ Does the Mission Statement set the company apart from the competition?

___ Is the Mission Statement ambitious enough?

___ Am I excited about the Mission Statement?

Understand that it's vitally important to have a good Vision Statement that is backed up by a comprehensive Mission Statement. But that's not the end of the story because, just like different countries, businesses need to operate within a specific culture. You see, countries have rules and regulations that their citizens collectively establish (through democratic means in most civilized countries), yet they go about their daily lives according to the culture that they happen to have. This means that, while the Italians and the English might both have similar rules and regulations that govern them, they go about their daily lives entirely differently. They eat different food, they speak different languages, and they have different moral codes of conduct. The English, for example, would find it rude to talk loudly in public, whereas the Italians certainly wouldn't. The Spanish don't consider it rude to interrupt while someone is talking, whereas the English do.

Think of a company's culture in much the same way. It's the way the members of that company go about meeting their objectives. It is their guide regarding all those unwritten, yet important, social issues that help give a business its character. It is that guide that lets team members know what is acceptable and what is not. It is a collection of values that lets every team member know what is most important in terms of thoughts and behavior.

Now, here's another thing you need to bear in mind; most companies don't have their culture written down so that everyone knows precisely what's expected of them.

Did you know that, unlike not having the Vision and Mission Statements, every company actually *has* a culture?

You see, if you don't proactively decide what your company's culture is going to be, your team members will do it for you. It will just happen; it will evolve over time all on its own. So my message to you is to take control and set one up with the help of your team. This is most important, as you'll want them to subscribe to it.

What types of things should you include in your Culture Statement? Well, it's generally a 12-point statement that includes the following:

Your three most important values as leader of the company.

Your team's three most important values.

Your customers' three most important values.

Your company's three most important values.

Here's what we have in place at **ActionCOACH.** Once again, it is discussed at length with all new team members at the time of their initial interview. Doing so saves us a whole lot of time and helps us find people who will fit in well with the rest of the team. We always find the right people from day one as a result.

This is our Culture Statement:

# *Action's* 14 Points of Culture

**1. Commitment**
I give myself and everything I commit to 100 percent until I succeed. I am committed to the Vision, Mission, Culture, and success of **ActionCOACH,** its current and future team, and its clients at all times. You will always recommend products and services of **ActionCOACH** prior to going outside the company.

**2. Ownership**
I am truly responsible for my actions and outcomes and own everything that takes place in my work and my life. I am accountable for my results and I know that for things to change, first I must change.

**3. Integrity**
I always speak the truth. What I promise is what I deliver. I only ever make agreements with myself and others that I am willing and intend to keep. I communicate any potential broken agreements at the first opportunity and I clear up all broken agreements immediately.

**4. Excellence**
Good enough isn't. I always deliver products and services of exceptional quality that add value to all involved for the long term. I look for ways to do more with less and stay on a path of constant and never-ending improvement and innovation.

**5. Communication**
I speak positively of my fellow team members, my clients, and **ActionCOACH** in both public and private. I speak with good purpose using empowering and

positive conversation. I never use or listen to sarcasm or gossip. I acknowledge what is being said as true for the speaker at that moment and I take responsibility for responses to my communication. I greet and say goodbye to people using their names. I always apologize for any upsets first and then look for a solution. I only ever discuss concerns in private with the person involved.

**6. Success**

I totally focus my thoughts, energy, and attention on the successful outcome of whatever I am doing. I am willing to win and allow others to win: Win/Win. At all times, I display my inner pride, prosperity, competence, and personal confidence. I am a successful person.

**7. Education**

I learn from my mistakes. I consistently learn, grow, and master so that I can help my fellow team members and clients learn, grow, and master too. I am an educator and allow my clients to make their own intelligent decisions about their future, remembering that it is their future. I impart practical and useable knowledge rather than just theory.

**8. Teamwork**

I am a team player and team leader. I do whatever it takes to stay together and achieve team goals. I focus on cooperation and always come to a resolution, not a compromise. I am flexible in my work and able to change if what I'm doing is not working. I ask for help when I need it and am compassionate to others who ask me.

**9. Balance**

I have a balanced approach to life, remembering that my spiritual, social, physical, and family aspects are just as important as my financial and intellectual. I complete my work and my most important tasks first, so I can have quality time to myself, with my family, and also to renew.

**10. Fun**

I view my life as a journey to be enjoyed and appreciated and I create an atmosphere of fun and happiness so all around me enjoy it as well.

**11. Systems**

I always look to the system for a solution. If a challenge arises I use a system correction before I look for a people correction. I use a system solution in my innovation rather than a people solution. I follow the system exactly until a new system is introduced. I suggest system improvements at my first opportunity.

**12. Consistency**
I am consistent in my actions so my clients and teammates can feel comfortable in dealing with me at all times. I am disciplined in my work so my results, growth, and success are consistent.

**13. Gratitude**
I am a truly grateful person. I say thank-you and show appreciation often and in many ways, so that all around me know how much I appreciate everything and everyone I have in my life. I celebrate my wins and the wins of my clients and team. I consistently catch myself and other people doing things right.

**14. Abundance**
I am an abundant person. I deserve my abundance and I am easily able to both give and receive it. I allow abundance in all areas of my life by respecting my own self-worth and that of all others. I am rewarded to the level that I create abundance for others, and I accept that abundance only shows up in my life to the level at which I show up.

When thinking about what values you'd like to encourage in your business, take a moment to answer the following questions:

1. In order to fulfill our Mission, what are the most important characteristics each team member must have?
2. What must we as an organization focus on to be our very best?
3. What qualities must we look for in the people we hire? Which qualities do you want each team member to value the most?
4. What are the characteristics that would conflict with the organization as it fulfils the Mission?

Are you beginning to see the importance and value of having in place good Vision, Mission, and Culture Statements? Can you see how these set the tone of the business and affect the types of people who will be attracted to your business?

# Part 2

## Putting Together the Dream Team

Before we consider ways of ensuring you have the team of your dreams in your business, let's consider for a moment just what a team is. According to the dictionary, a team is "a group of people who are on the same side." It is also "a group organized to work together." But there's more. In old English, the word refers to offspring or family. Isn't that interesting?

In my business, my team is considered part of my family. You should consider yours to be too. You see, if you regard your team members as family, you'll treat them a whole lot differently than what you would if they were just "staff," wouldn't you? Think about it. You may have noticed I never refer to my people as staff; they are members of my team.

Here's another meaning of the word team: *T*ogether *E*veryone *A*chieves *M*ore.

The overall feeling here is one of togetherness. The word conjures up an impression of inclusiveness. And this is important, because when you really think about it, everyone in your company has a unique and equally important role. None is more important than the others. They all have a distinct purpose that plays an important role in the overall well-being of your business. If they didn't, then there's something wrong with your structure. You see, in business there should be no freeloaders. Everyone should have a unique and distinct role to play in helping the company achieve its Goals, Mission, and Vision. It's as simple as that.

But there's another dimension here that needs to be highlighted. Team members not only have to fulfil a particular function within the organization, they also have to fit in with the rest of the team as far as compatibility is concerned. You know the old saying that one rotten apple spoils the basket? Well, it's true in business. It all comes down to your company's culture. Finding the right match is vitally important when selecting team members. That's why I involve my entire team when looking for a new team member. You see, team members are the ones who have to live and work with the new team member, not I.

So how should you go about ensuring that you match the members of your team up well with each other? The first thing to do is to consider the different behavioral styles people have. I do this by means of the DISC Personality Profile.

## DISC Personality Profile

It would help if we were able to understand, in broad terms, the way people behave towards each other. Understanding this would make our lives very much easier when it comes to interacting with them.

One system I recommend is the DISC Personality Profile. The American Psychologist Dr. William Moulton Marsden designed this system back in the 1920s. It places people into one of four different personality types, or categories; D—Dominant, I—Influential, S—Steady, and C—Compliant.

The DISC Personality Profile is an accurate personality analysis that can be used to predict the behavior of individuals when they work on their own and with others. However, this system is not infallible. Like anything, it has its limitations. Its shortfall is that people seldom have just one personality. They are, rather, a combination of the four, just in different ratios. Everyone is dominant in one personality type, but another may be closely following.

The DISC test highlights a person's relative strengths in each of the four areas—Outgoing or Reserved, and Task Oriented or People Oriented. The area that scores highest will be the person's dominant trait.

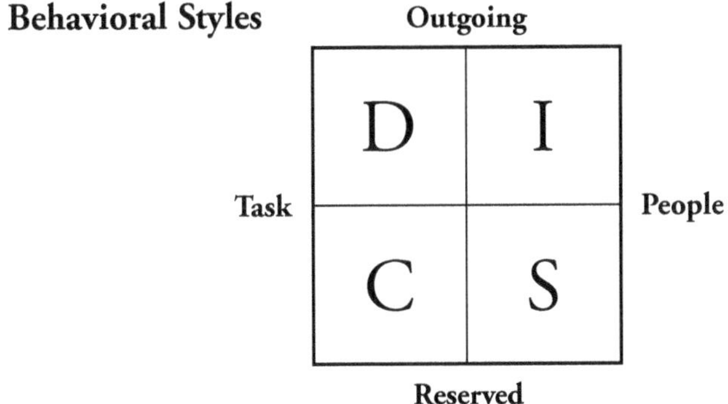


The results aren't always accurate, especially when the people being tested are aware of their personality eccentricities and have moved to improve these traits. The higher the strength shown from the test, the more the descriptions will fit. Don't use this as a definitive method for labelling people's traits. Use it as a guide to communicating with them.

Everyone has weaknesses, and this system is meant as a guide to identify them. Remember, if you are happy as you are, that's great.

When you read the characteristics of the various personality types, you will start to understand how people can be expected to behave when you interact with them.

## High I Personalities

High I's like to have fun and be popular. You can recognize them by their outgoing and very friendly manner. They want to be people's friends. They will rarely tell anyone off. When they say something in anger, they don't want you to remind them of it again because that was in the past and they really weren't that serious when they said it in the first place.

High I's don't like to get into too much detail as they don't find that fun. They like to work with others in a changing environment. High I's can be recognized by their very friendly disposition. They look you in the eye and usually use a lot of tonal changes in their voices.

They talk a bit louder than other personality types, except the High D, who can also talk confidently and loudly. This is the mark of an extrovert. The difference between them is that High I's are loud and friendly. If you joke with either of them, a High I will respond but a High D may not.

High I's will respond more quickly because they think you're like them, so they'll let you know by giving you a friendly response.

## High I Interaction

High I's get on fairly well with most personality types. They can annoy the High C and High D because they're task-oriented and just want to get the job done without being friendly while doing it. All the other personality types can see a High I as overly friendly. They might say, "Mellow out a bit. You come on too strong and annoy people. Don't be so friendly."

High I's are good motivators and team leaders although they won't like pulling team members into line if they've done something they shouldn't have.

## Managing the High I

To manage High I's you need to win them over and be their friend. If you don't show you care about them or that you like them, they won't want to work with you.

You need to show that you have a sense of humor, are a fun-loving person, and you are having fun talking to them right now. You can work on being a little bit stern but not too serious.

High I's want to do what seems popular. They don't want to do anything that seems like detailed work that will take up lots of their time. If it seems boring to them, they won't want it. The best thing you can say to them is that it will be a lot of fun.

They will work well with people who seem to have the same nature as they do. So be happy and spontaneous. Talk about other things apart from work. Get chatty at the start, during the middle, and the end of the work process. They will sometimes want to go off on a tangent. Let them do most of the talking. They love to talk about anything, especially other people.

Be their friend and advise them on what you think and feel is best for them. Be sincere. Be like them and they will love you.

If you're a High D, don't talk too much. Let them decide that they want the system and that it seems like a popular idea and makes sense. High D's need to be friendlier than they usually are when in the work place.

You can't be too friendly with High I's—as long as you're sincere. They are people's people and have great people skills. They won't like you if you are fake.

High I's are prone to exaggerate. They like to tell stories, and you can too when working with them. But tell them if you are exaggerating.

### Areas They Need to Work On

High I's need to work on getting the job done and not being distracted by other people. They need to be more task oriented. They need to get into the details more, as this is what they don't like doing.

They need to be less extroverted with people, especially High C's and High S's. When communicating with High C's they don't need to be their friends, which is what they believe.

High I's are a bit too friendly for the High S, although the High S can see that aspect of them and not let it bother them. High I's need to recognize that the other personality types are not like them. They also need to work on being more like the others when communicating with them.

## High D Personalities

High D's like to be in control. They want to be at the top and give the orders. They have a hard time following orders, as they feel their own way is always better. High D's will usually end up in management positions, self-employed, or in charge of a section that has a bit of room to move unsupervised.

They like to be in control of their own lives and make their own decisions. High D's can seem to be too powerful or too strong for other people. They are confident, outspoken, and say what they feel. This can offend others, as they can be thought of as arrogant. They aren't usually; it's just the way they express themselves.

High D's have active minds that like to be stimulated; they like to be doing lots of things at once. When they do more than one thing at a time, the quality can start to drop. It can be difficult for them to follow something to its end. They feel a great need for lots of activity. When you want something done in a hurry, give it to a High D.

## High D Interaction

High D's do not interact well with others. They give orders and like to take control, and this can detract from their relationships with others.

High D's can sabotage or undermine the authority of High I's and not be at all worried about it affecting their popularity. While the High I likes to have fun working with a group, the High D isn't that interested, or at least not to the same degree.

Often High D's have a lot of High I in them; they just need to tap into it a bit more to get along better with a High I.

A High D works well with a High C. Neither needs to be friendly while working, so they get the job done. The two personalities compliment each other very well. The High D gets on best with a High C. A High D likes to delegate, and the best one to delegate to is the High C.

However, because the High D is not detail-oriented and the High C is, a problem can occur. The High C will need lots of details on how to do something, and this is precisely something the High D doesn't like to give.

Also High C's prefer to do the same thing over and over. They like doing what they know how to do. That's often how they get their significance and feelings of importance, by doing something perfectly.

A High D gets along reasonably well with and a High S because the latter is steadying, reserved, and tolerant of others. High S's do not need to be given the details like a High C does. They can just be told what to do and they do it.

High S's know that High D's like to control others and don't let it worry them. High D's don't consider their mode of interaction, like needing to relay instructions with details for the High C, or with friendliness to a High I, so the High S works best with a High D.

High D's may think High S's are inferior because they mistake their natural reserve and steadiness with lacking in confidence. Often High S's have great self-confidence; they just don't need to display it like a High D does. High D's like confident people, as they can relate better to them.

### Managing the High D

High D's like to be leaders. They like to do what no one else is doing. They like to be innovative pioneers. The best way to work with them is to tell them that they need to be more productive, profitable, successful, and a leader of others.

Respect them and never make them feel inferior. They need to respect the manager. Most importantly, they need to be confident that you can deliver what you say you can. They need to be given the facts and reasons. Also don't try and be too friendly to them.

They want a summary of any features the new system may have. They don't need details; in fact going over details annoys them. Give a brief outline of different things showing the logic of it all. They want to be productive, so tell them what you have will help their cause. Tell them they will be more successful using the new system. That's what they want to know.

Give them better solutions or ways of doing things. Be blunt if you have to; they don't mind too much and they don't care—but only if they have your respect.

### Areas They Need to Work On

The major area they need to work on is their people skills and communication with others. They also need to slow down to check if they are making progress. When talking to a High C, they need to give more specifics.

They need to be friendlier to others they work with. They need to have a checking system on their progress and of how well they are doing. Are the jobs they start being completed, and if so, how good is the quality? They need to stop, plan, and think more before they start, and also as they progress.

## High S Personalities

High S's are steady people. They don't like to rush things. When everyone else is stressing out, they remain calm. They like to plod along, thinking things over before doing anything. They don't like making quick decisions.

They are well liked by all personality types because they are friendly, easy-going, and harmless. People admire their cool disposition. They just get in and get the job done, although usually not at a great pace.

While High D's start going flat out without knowing if they are doing it right, the High I gets everyone together so they can all get involved and have fun. The High C plans every detail meticulously before making a start, while the High S thinks it over for a fair while before making a slow start.

## High S Interaction

High S's get on well with High D's because they probably understand them and it doesn't worry them when the High D gives orders. Because High S's are calm, they are a help to the High D.

High S's can plan things, which is a help to the High D. They slow the High D down, and this can be both a good thing and a bad. High D's often end up marrying High S's.

The High S gets along well with the High I. They are both people-oriented. The High S is a calmer, more reserved version of the High I. The High S might say to the High I, "Mellow out. You come on too strong. You're too friendly." While the High I will respond, "Get a bit more life in you."

They both have fun in life, or try to. The High S has a high concern for others and tries to understand them. When High I's work with High S's, they can often get carried away with having fun, as they're not as task-oriented as the High D and High C.

The two usually won't get as much done as the other two personality types.

High S's and High C's are both introverted. They both like to take their time in making a decision. They work well together, although they won't get a task done as quickly as the D's and I's. They will think about it for a while first.

The High S will feel there's no need to rush into it. High C's will agree because they will want to consider all the details before they start anyway. High C's will be planning it out perfectly before they start, and if it's taking too long to start, the High S's won't say too much because they like to keep the peace.

However, the two personality types will get a job done well together and it will be done correctly.

The High D and High S get a job done well and compliment each other nicely. The High S will bring the High D's feet back down to earth and steady them. The High D will speed up the High S's' decision-making process, which is sometimes needed.

The High S admires the High D's leadership ability, while the High D admires the High S's steadiness—although not always. Because the High S is reserved while the High D is outgoing, they learn from each other in different situations.

### Managing the High S

They are harder to work with than the High D or High I. They like to be steady in their decision making. They don't like to rush anything. They like to take their time in reaching a decision. They don't like pressure or pushy people.

You need to be their friend and build genuine rapport with them. Be reserved like they are. Be casual. Outline what you want them to do, and then give details. Give them data to make a decision and tell them they need to make it soon.

Don't expect quick decisions, though. Explain at the start that if you can give them everything they want and expect today, and you both agree it's the best thing, then you'll outline the steps needed to get the process underway. Then ask if it's OK to do that. Get them to commit to making a decision then and there if you can.

Sometimes High S's won't make a decision at all on the same day. If that's the case, be aware that it often happens. Give them some time and get back to them the next day. Be firm in wanting a decision soon (or today), but don't be pushy.

Be reserved like they are. High S's don't like change. Give them plenty of eye contact. Build rapport and be their friend.

### Areas They Need to Work On

High S's need to work on changing their ways more quickly. They change in time, however, they are the most reluctant of all personality types to do so. High D's will change before you finish telling them why they need to. To High I's change is fun. They like change because they like variety in their lives.

High C's won't usually change much at all. This is because they have just finished learning how to do something the best way they can, and now they just want to keep doing it. They love getting into a routine and staying that way. How can you achieve perfection in anything if you don't stick to it for ages?

High S's need to practice making quick decisions and not looking back once they've made the decision. They need to realize that often a quick decision is better than no decision at all.

## High C Personalities

High C's are interesting in many ways. They have a tendency to collect data, facts, and figures. They can often stutter their words when describing things, possibly due to tension, and also because they are thinking what the perfect way to describe this is. High C's often stutter more than other personality types.

High C's like to do things very well, if not perfectly. However, they don't reference their standards to others, which would be valuable to them because then they would learn that their standards are much higher than everyone else's.

They often create stress in their lives by this ongoing striving to live up to their own perfect standards. They can miss out on seeing the big picture, as they can get stuck on the details.

They want to work on their own because they feel they will do the job best. They think other people won't do as good a job as they will. High C's are reserved and task-oriented, which means they aren't that friendly in communication with other people, especially nonfamily and friends.

They like to give lots of data when they communicate, as they feel this is what people want.

They can have high levels of stress due to rarely being able to live up to their own high standards. They like to have many details before making a decision. They virtually never rush into anything, especially without considering all the facts, data, and graphs. Then they like to think more on it.

They don't like to be pushed into doing things, as they feel their way is nearly always the best. They like to plan things out before lifting a finger. Conditions usually have to be perfect before they proceed.

## High C Interaction

High C's complement a High D because they are virtual opposites; one is introverted and the other is extroverted. The High C is reserved while the High D is outgoing. Both are task-oriented.

High C's get self-satisfaction and pride from doing things for others. Although if they don't know how to do what the High D is asking, there can be problems.

The High C needs to be shown in detail how to do something. The High D isn't into details, so a communication problem can occur. For this pairing to work, High D's need to explain in more detail how to do the things they want done.

High C's and High I's are interesting combinations. They can work well together, although they can often have troubles. When they struggle in relationships, it can be due to their opposite natures. A High I is extroverted, while a High C is introverted.

A High I person is people-oriented while a High C is task-oriented. These traits can cause a lot of conflict. The High I will say or think that the High C is spending too much time on unimportant things. The High C may think the High I is flaky and doesn't work on what is really important.

The High C will want the High I to be less friendly and more task oriented, while the High I will think the opposite.

As a working combination, the two are good for each other if they can put aside their differences. High I's will stop the High C's from being introverted and get them to have more fun and work with others. The High C will bring the High I's back down to earth and get them working on the details. As a combination in business, they can work well together.

## Managing the High C

Managing a High C can be challenging. High C's can be very skeptical of anyone in authority, because they often feel they know it all already.

They can often resist change because they have their own way of doing things. They won't consider accepting better or different ways of doing things unless you show them the facts—the facts must be valid and there must be lots of them.

Be prepared to spend a lot of time with them. They will ask a hundred questions and procrastinate because they will be wondering whether they've covered every detail they need to know about.

They will be wary of change agents. This is mainly because they have found how to do things without anyone's help, and new ways of doing things will mean they'll need to relearn. They're much happier doing what they already know how to do.

They aren't overly friendly like the High I and High S. You can't just tell them that they need to do things your way like you can the High D. They only want one thing—data. So give them as much data as you can. And give it in graph, table, written, or essay form.

You can't give High C's too much data to consider. They like to justify their decisions by logic. They don't care if you are their best friend—they always consider the facts first.

Don't expect High C's to make quick decisions. They like time to think. So give it to them. Talk about facts backed up by logic. Get back to them another day only if you tell them you've given them everything they need to make a decision.

They are confident in their own abilities and are used to relying on making their own decisions. They will talk confidently because they have a lot of knowledge and are proud of it. If you tell them that you have a way of helping them do things better and more efficiently, you will get their attention eventually. Anything that improves their standards or efficiency they will love. Tell them they'll be able to do even better with this.

### Areas They Need to Work On

Their own standards can be too high compared to others. They can be stressed people due to their feeling that everything they do needs to be perfect. This is the standard they always strive for. It can come from the fact they don't realize their standards are already far above anyone else's.

They need to get someone else's opinion when working on a task and accept their standards as being good enough. A High C needs to strive for excellence, not perfection!

Most High C's think they can do a better job, and often they can. But usually the standard a High C works to is the minority's opinion because everyone else acknowledges excellence while a High C keeps on chasing perfection. High C's need to stop at excellence.

They need to work more with others to get used to their level of excellence, and then to accept it as their own "new" standard.

High C's needs to be more confident in their approach to decision making and not fear arriving at a wrong decision. After all, High D's make decisions a lot more quickly than a High C ever will. High D's far, far, outweigh High C's when it comes to successful people. So High C's need to get into the habit of making quicker decisions so they can develop a better, stronger, emotional muscle.

High C's need to do things that are new or different. They need to forget their schedules. Throw it away for a day. Do something spontaneous. Do something on the spur of the moment. Do something because it looks like fun. They need to tell themselves that change is fun, that it is good. They need to be more spontaneous.

They also need to get more help from others. They need to ask themselves if what they are doing is the most important thing they could be doing. Will spending the time doing it perfectly really benefit them or others, or should they say, "This is excellent, what can I do next?"

High C's need to move on more. They need to get more involved with people. They need to open up and tell others what they are feeling. A very wise man once said, "Vulnerability is strength because you open yourself up to change and improvement."

High C's need to be spontaneous more often. They need to take on more like a High D does. They need to do more things at once so they don't get stuck on the details that aren't always important.

## People under Pressure

To better understand this section, remember the four main personality types: D—Dominant, I—Influential, S—Steady, and C—Compliant.

People can change their natures under pressure. High I's can become High S's under pressure. This means that they slow down and think more; they become more reserved.

High I's can become High D's, which means instead of being friendly to everyone, they start to boss everyone around without much regard for their feelings. People around them would wonder what happened to that friendly person who got on with everyone so well.

High D's can become High C's under pressure. They will now consider details more and think carefully before making a decision. High D's could go to High S's, meaning they will steady themselves and slow down. They will consider the people around them more.

High S's could even become High D's under pressure. They now have to act and think quickly when placed under lots of pressure. They might start to become loud and bark out orders when normally they are calm, reserved, and friendly.

High C's could move to High D's under pressure. They will think and act more quickly than previously, making decisions quickly without considering all the details. You've heard people say they work best under pressure; this could mean that they've become a High D under pressure to get more done.

Normally a High C wouldn't change to a High I or High S under pressure, or a High I wouldn't go to a High C under pressure, as these two personality types are so different.

Often a person stays the same under pressure. A High D can stay a High D. A High S can stay a High S, and so on. Not everyone changes under pressure. You will know when someone does. It will be quite noticeable.

## Making Sense out of This

The DISC profile gives you a very good indication of people's behavioral styles at work. It's a very good idea to assess each member of your existing team, as well as prospective new members so that you can obtain a better or clearer understanding of the different styles you're dealing with. Contact your nearest *Action* Business Coach if you need to run these assessments. They are also widely available from various sources.

The idea here is to try and match up the predominant style of the new applicant with those of the rest of your team. You see, expecting two people with incompatible styles to work harmoniously together is asking for trouble. Try rather to aim for compatibility in the first place.

Much depends, of course, on the type of job the new person will be doing—whether it is a management role or a support function, or whether there is much team interaction or not. So pay attention to the results of the applicant's DISC profile. You will be able to make an educated or informed judgment based on this.

You will also have a very good idea of the type of person you'd like to fill the role; you might want an extrovert to fill a salesperson's role, for instance. By asking applicants to complete a DISC profile, you'll get a very good idea of how suitable they will be as far as this goes.

But it's not just a person's characteristics *at work* that are important; what you should be considering is the *entire* personality of the person. This means that you need to pay some attention to what I call their Living Styles as well as their Working Styles. You see, people do have two distinct "personalities"—the one they want to expose to the world while at work (their professional style) and the style they have at home. A good example of this is a receptionist's "office" voice. Have you ever noticed how they seem to have two very different voices? The one they use when answering the office phone is very different than the one that they use when talking to a friend on the phone. This is only natural, but if you want to assemble your dream team, you really need to know what people are like in their private lives as well as in their professional lives.

Now, I'm not suggesting you need to pry into their private lives at all. What I mean by private life is actually their "real" personalities. Understand that when at work they will only be exposing their persona, not their true personality. Finding compatible team members means matching them up according to their real personalities, not their personas.

Let me show you what I mean.

People have different Living Styles based on where they lie on a scale that measures four characteristics; high or low self-respect, and high or low respect for others. It's that simple. Where they fit in this table will indicate their relationship with others in their private lives. This is what I mean: (see the following table)

## Living Styles

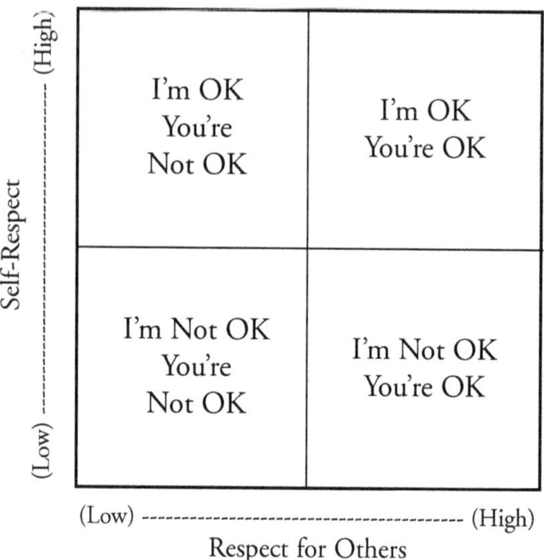


Working Styles are based on the same characteristics, but in the workplace. Where they lie on this table will indicate broadly what their relationship with their coworkers will be. This is what I mean:

## Working Styles

| Self-Respect (Low) ------ (High) | | |
|---|---|---|
| (High) | Hostile/ Aggressive<br>WIN : LOSE | Assertive<br>WIN : WIN |
| (Low) | Manipulative/ Aggressive<br>LOSE : LOSE | Passive<br>LOSE : WIN |
| | (Low) | (High) |

(Low) ------------------------------------------ (High)
Respect for Others

So how do you go about assessing someone's Living and Working Styles? Simple. You assess them subjectively according to the two main criteria. Try it and you'll see it's really quite easy to do. You can easily and quickly get a rough idea while talking informally to people, whether they generally have a higher or lower respect for themselves and for others. Of course, the more you practice it, the better you will become at it.

Once you have done this, compare all three results together. Consider the results obtained from the DISC Profile with their Living Style and their Working Style, and you'll begin to form a very good idea of the people. It will be an easy task now to determine whether those people would fit in well with the rest of your team.

Remember, one's private and business lives are a mirror of each other—you attract only what you deserve.

Part 3

# Six Keys to a Winning Team

Selecting the right people is but the start of building a successful team for your business. It's just one of the many ingredients that contribute towards the making of a dream team.

It's one thing to have great people working for you; it's another to have all the other important elements in place so that this team can become a winning team.

You simply can't expect your team alone to transform your business. There are other factors that come into play. Fortunately, these factors are controllable. It's up to you to ensure that they compliment your team.

So, what are these factors? I'll run through them one by one.

## Strong Leadership

If your dream team isn't backed up and guided by strong leadership, the result will be like having a supertanker sailing the ocean without a rudder. Strong leadership is crucial. Of course, by strong leader I don't mean an autocrat or a dictator. There may well be instances where this type of leadership style is appropriate, such as in a takeover or merger between two companies, but generally speaking, a strong leader is something quite different. Understand that I'm not referring solely to the style of leadership here. I'm talking more about the quality of leadership.

Let's look at this a bit more closely.

### Different Styles of Leadership

Consider first the two basic types of leader. I'm talking in general terms here. What two stereotypes spring immediately to mind?

Most people will say the tough, no-nonsense type and the easygoing type. And they would be right.

I'm sure you will have come across many examples of these two styles. We all know what type Army Sergeant Majors are, don't we!

The first dimension along which leadership style is defined ranges from democratic to autocratic. The democratic leader is one who involves others in the leadership decision-making process, whereas the autocratic leader doesn't. Most leaders fall somewhere in the middle of these two extremes. They fall somewhere along the Democratic–Autocratic scale.

Of course, this is a simplistic view of leadership style. Life just isn't so clear-cut. What other major characteristics could be used to identify leadership styles? What other dimension should we judge it on? This other dimension characterises leadership styles according to the degree to which they concentrate on task behavior or relationship behavior.

What does this mean?

When a leader gets involved with the team members, telling them exactly what to do and when, how to do it, and where it should be done, that's a good example of task behavior. The main concern of the leader here is getting the job done. Relationship behavior, on the other hand, has more to do with explaining, listening, encouraging, supporting, and generally facilitating team members when they go about tackling their tasks. Can you see the difference?

Leadership styles can now be better represented by considering all four types together. They can also be graphically represented by means of the following diagram:

## Leadership Styles

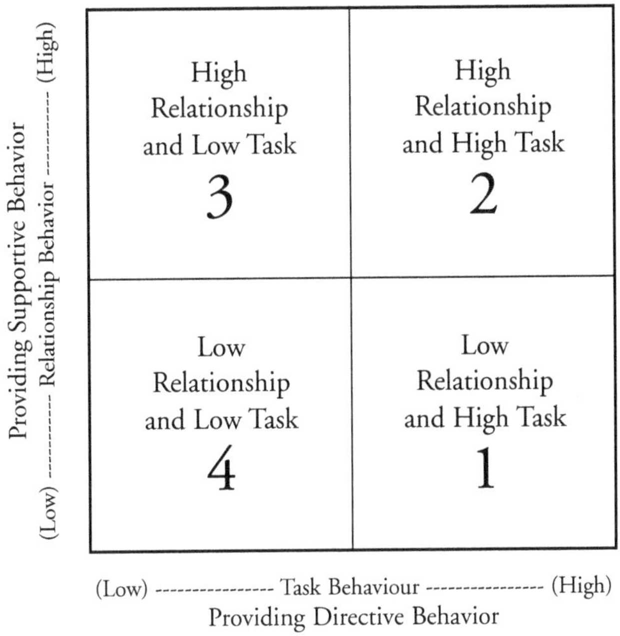

| | | |
|---|---|---|
| (High) Providing Supportive Behavior / Relationship Behavior | High Relationship and Low Task 3 | High Relationship and High Task 2 |
| (Low) | Low Relationship and Low Task 4 | Low Relationship and High Task 1 |

(Low) --------------- Task Behaviour --------------- (High)
Providing Directive Behavior

From this you can see that some managers will concentrate more on task-related behavior and not on relationship behavior (Style 1) while those characterized as Style 2 will display high task and relationship behaviors. Style 3 leaders display high relationship behavior and low task behavior, while Style 4 leaders are low in both task and relationship behavior.

Understand that there are no right or wrong leadership styles. You don't have to go about changing your style just because you might be a Style 4 person. There is a place in business for all styles. Consider the situation where you have a really efficient, experienced store person whom you know you can rely on at all times. In this case Style 4 would be totally appropriate, wouldn't it? Interfering too much (by adopting a Style 1 approach, for instance) would prove counterproductive, as your store person would feel you no longer trust the standard of work she was performing. She would feel you were interfering in her job, wouldn't she?

The important point here is you should adapt your leadership style to suit not only the current situation but also the situation as it evolves. You might, for instance, use a Style 1 approach when starting a new business, then switching to Style 2 as the business establishes itself. You see, your team members will have become a lot more confident and comfortable in their jobs, but they would still require a high level of task behavior input from you. They will now be needing more relationship behavior input. They will appreciate more emotional support, positive feedback, and encouragement. Then as they become proficient in their jobs, they will flourish by being allowed to "run their own shows" without interference. However, they will still require a high level of relationship behavior input from you. This will do wonders for their confidence levels, which in turn will produce results for your bottom line. Finally, Style 4 will be appropriate when your business and your team could be considered mature. They will need little in the way of supportive behavior from you. A good example of this situation is when the owner of the business has stepped aside from the business, allowing the business to run itself.

The leader needs to assess the situation and bring the appropriate style to the situation. If, for instance, you had a mature business in which you generally employed a Style 4 type of leadership, and you now wanted to introduce systems to run the business, you'd probably change to a Style 2 for the duration of the installation process, then change to a Style 3 while the team gets used to the systems, then finally back to a Style 4 once the team has been properly installed, tested, and measured, and the team is totally comfortable with the leadership.

## Passion and Responsibility

The hallmark of a strong leader is passion and responsibility. These two qualities really set them apart from ordinary or situational leaders. People always respond well to leaders who are passionate about their jobs, their businesses, or their lives. It's contagious; the team members will find themselves motivated to perform at their very best when led by a passionate leader.

Of course, it's one thing to be passionate about what you are doing, but passion alone won't make you a strong leader. There's another quality that must go with it, and that's responsibility. You see, a strong leader is one who will also accept responsibility for the actions of the entire team. It's absolutely essential that the leader is able to make decisions in a decisive manner. This means assuming responsibility for the decisions made and the consequences that flow as a result. It's the ability to follow through that counts—being able to see the consequences of managerial decisions through to the very end and to assume full responsibility for them.

## 16 Cylinders of High Performance

There's another concept of strong leadership I'd like to introduce here. It's what I call the *16 Cylinders of High Performance.* Imagine the people you're about to lead, each being represented by a massive 16-cylinder engine. Ask yourself how many cylinders each person is currently running on. Some will be running on four, some on eight. Now, in order to get each and every one of them running on all 16, we need to understand how human beings are built.

We all have four main segments: body, mind, heart, and spirit.

The average organization only recognizes the first two in its leaders. Some even tell them to leave their emotional stuff at home. It's very important to understand body and mind only have, in my analogy, three cylinders each. This would mean in these types of organizations, their leaders are firing only on six cylinders and not all 16. These six cover the sorts of things you read about people on their resumes. But if you think about it, the more important things are heart and spirit, which, in my analogy have five cylinders each. They are the attributes that tell you whether a person has the drive, the passion, and the get-up-and-go for the job.

When you have a leader who is firing on all 16 cylinders, you'll be absolutely amazed at the results. This is because there will now be synergy in the team. Understand this: the synergy in a team is one of the things that will jump your business to a level you never expected. But more about this later.

## Perturbation

Managers tend to concentrate more on the technical side of business, directing people on the job, making sure tasks are done to predetermined standards or expectations, and ensuring that deadlines are met. This is why I call them technicians. You see, what they are most concerned with are those aspects that I class as body and mind. They concentrate on their team members' technical abilities and skills. Remember, these account for only three cylinders each in my 16-cylinder analogy. This means that the typical manager is only firing on six cylinders of the available 16.

However, as they develop and grow—as they become leaders—they will find their roles have changed significantly. No longer will they be operating like a technician; they will be delegating that responsibility to someone else. And this won't come easy. You see, they will first have to learn to let go—to trust someone else. This "grey area" or uncertain territory that they will move into will certainly be outside their comfort zones. They will find themselves in an unhappy and worried mental state. This is what is known as perturbation. Think of it as an activity they'd view, initially at least, as an intrusion.

The symptom of the shift from Manager to Leader is perturbation.

The difference between a Manager and a Leader is really that the Leader takes a far greater interest in those areas I call heart and spirit. These are the emotional aspects of the team members, and they account for five cylinders each in my 16-cylinder analogy. The strong leader fires on all 16 cylinders.

### Cycles of Business

So what does all this actually mean as far as your business is concerned? Well, everything really. You see, there's no substitute for strong leadership. Little can usually be achieved without the cooperation of others. As a leader, you must create excellent people in your business. You must help them to grow so your business can grow. By inspiring and encouraging them, they will in turn inspire and encourage your customers, who will bring in the business.

Keep your team's knowledge updated and work harder on yourself than on your job. Remember, you always get the people you deserve. Become a great leader and you will get great people. Learn to think outside the box. Walk the walk; don't just talk the talk.

## Common Goal

The next thing you need to do is to set a common goal. You need to tell your team members what the goal of your business is. You can't expect them to achieve results if they don't know what the overall goal is that they must be aiming for.

It all starts with your Vision. The Vision must be regarded as the central aim that enrolls the support of all your team members. It inspires them to do the things they have to do to meet their own individual goals.

From the Vision, you develop your Mission Statement. Your goals are very much more specific activities that, when achieved, help you accomplish your mission and fulfil your vision.

By setting goals, you give your business direction and focus as well as movement and momentum. They are the things that get the business moving. Everyone needs to have goals that collectively help the business progress in the direction of its ultimate vision. It's no use setting individual goals for team members that pull in opposite directions. You'll be surprised at how easy this is to do. For example, a factory owner might set his production manager the goal of operating with no overtime, yet he might set his salespeople the goal of doubling the sales of widgets, even though it is only possible to produce the additional items by operating shifts on overtime.

So, make sure you set *smart* goals. What are these? They are Specific, Measurable, Achievable, Results-oriented goals that have a Time Frame. If your goals don't meet these basic criteria, they won't be of much use. You or your team won't be able to achieve them. They will be unrealistic and a waste of time.

## Rules of the Game

You must set the rules of the game. You must tell your team members what they can and can't do. You need to create the playing field. All team members must know the rules, which must be written down and available. You see, if you don't give them the rules, they'll go outside the boundaries.

These detail the standards and norms. And remember, your rules will affect your culture, and *vice versa*.

You must aim at establishing tight points of culture, or boundaries, across which your team members are not allowed to venture. Within these boundaries they can move about as they please. I call this a Loose/Tight Culture. Think of it like a game of football. As long as you obey the rules of the game, you can move about the playing field wherever you like. You are loosely regulated within the tightly bound playing field.

This is a marvelous setup for any business to have, yet you'd be surprised at how many don't have any delineated boundaries at all. This forces them to have a multitude of individual work contracts to regulate each individual team member. You see, if they didn't, chaos would reign. But by having to rely on this tightly regulated setup within the playing field, most businesses sacrifice internal harmony, creativity, and team spirit. It's certainly a less than ideal situation that relies on policing instead of trust.

Remember, if you don't establish your company's culture, your team will do it for you. You will end up with a *de facto* culture that most probably won't be to your liking or in the best interests of your company.

## Action Plan

Every business needs an *Action* plan. The first thing you need to do here is to give all team members a position description. They need to know what their jobs entail and what their responsibilities are. It's very important to tell your people what they're supposed to be doing. Spell it out in clear, unambiguous terms. There's nothing more daunting for new team members than arriving on their first day and being unsure about what they are expected to do. They will be confused enough without this added burden.

Having positional contracts will also save you the agony of sorting out involved and emotionally charged disputes that may arise through misunderstandings relating to what a person should or shouldn't be doing. This is particularly so when things go wrong in the workplace and fingers start being pointed.

The second thing you need to do is to develop a strategy that lays down how results are to be achieved and why certain things are done.

Third, you need a tactic that spells out how results will be achieved.

Once you've done that, you then need to develop systems by which your team can achieve results, and you need to tell them who is doing what by when. To find out more about this in detail, read my book *Instant Systems.*

Start off by documenting exactly what each person does on a daily, weekly, and monthly basis. I'll cover this again in more detail in Part 5.

Once you have done that, you can bind all the resultant documents together, sorted by functional area or department, and the result will be a complete systems manual for your business. I'll talk more about how you go about writing the systems manuals in Part 5.

Understand that playing for a championship team means making sure you stay in position. After all, that is what you are accountable for, isn't it? This doesn't mean if someone asks for help, you don't give it. It means you come to a resolution so you can still get on with your job while assisting him in finding a solution to his particular challenge.

## Support Risk Taking

You must be willing to take risks. If you don't, your team will always lag behind and will not push boundaries. Remember, your business is just like a tree; it's either growing or it's dying. There's no middle ground. It can't stand still.

Most people don't like taking risks. They are risk averse. Why is this? It has a lot to do with their habits. You see, we do what we do because of well-ingrained habits. A habit is something we do automatically. But habits can be changed. It only takes 21 days to instill a new habit—that's all. Just concentrate on doing something in a different manner for 21 days and it will become a habit. Or concentrate on not doing something for 21 days and you'll lose the habit. Remember, a breakthrough usually follows a breakwith, a breakapart, a breakup, or a breakdown. Sometimes we need one of these things to happen before we can make a breakthrough in changing our ways.

It's also true that everyone can tolerate some level of risk. The level varies from person to person depending on the situation and the circumstances. This could involve financial investments, gambling, or looking for a new job. In fact, many will tell you that life itself is a risk.

Risk taking in business is slightly different in that it's usually tied up with the company's culture. If the owner doesn't encourage the team members to take business risks, the business will progress conservatively towards its goals. It will most probably make slow, unspectacular progress. It will also most likely project a dull image. Its people will behave themselves in an appropriate manner, not wanting to step out of line by pushing any boundaries. The company will most probably never develop anything unique and will shy away from operating at the leading edge. It will not be thought of as an innovator.

Some companies actually encourage their people to experiment with new ways of doing things. They reward their team members for innovation or improvements to the way they do things. Consequently, people who work for companies like this will feel invigorated, stimulated, and appreciated in the workplace. They will enjoy coming to work each day, because they will have tremendous job satisfaction. Chances are too that they will always be willing to go the extra mile without having to be asked. They will willingly give of their very best. They will portray, through their actions and reactions, the face of a happy, vibrant company. This will be picked up by their customers, who will readily prefer doing business with them.

Everyone likes being associated with winners, and it's no different in business. *Kaizen,* the Japanese concept of never-ending improvement, will be a living concept in the business, as team members will naturally be seeking to constantly improve the way they operate. Efficiency levels will go through the roof, with a corresponding increase being noticeable on the bottom line. Success becomes a self-fulfilling prophecy.

## 100 Percent Involvement/Inclusion

The final point concerning putting together a winning team draws the previous ones together. And if these have been implemented properly, it should happen automatically.

It's all about having each and every member of your team giving your business *all* of her attention, effort, and commitment.

You need to make sure everyone on the team is involved. And this involvement must be 100 percent by 100 percent of the team members. They all need to be firing on all 16 cylinders.

You must also practice the art of inclusion. Let me talk about sabotage to illustrate this point. If employees are trying to covertly sabotage your organization, they can easily do so just by not getting involved in the work situation. You can counter this by asking for their opinions and then listening to what they say. If, on the other hand, they wanted to overtly sabotage your business, they could do this by taking control. This is the biggest single stumbling block in team situations.

While on the topic of control, consider this: if the owners of a business think they need to control everything themselves, they will eventually lose control, as it's impossible to control anything but yourself. Their controlling tendencies will eventually destroy the business. As business owners, we must ask ourselves how we can run a business if we can't control it.

Part 4

# Getting the Environment Right

People are amazing—they will achieve extraordinary results if you let them. The people you work with can be far more effective if you create an environment where each helps the other create synergy. Without the people who can run your business, you'll trap yourself in the business forever.

Now here's something that might surprise you. I expect my people to be better than I am.

Surprised? You shouldn't be. Here's why.

With most people these days being taught from an early age to specialize, to follow orders, to conform, to fit in, and to get a good job with a good salary, we've created a monster when it comes to letting people start their own businesses.

You see, we've been taught to do the opposite of thinking for ourselves, of getting rich, and in most cases of learning how to be strong leaders and true entrepreneurs.

Let me give you a good example of what I'm talking about.

Most will agree that Henry Ford was a strong leader and a true entrepreneur. I'm sure this story I'm about to relate has changed a little over the years, but there's no doubt still a level of truth in it. As the story goes, a major newspaper defamed Mr. Ford by publishing an article that portrayed him as ignorant.

Mr. Ford took the newspaper to court and while on the stand, he was questioned at length by the newspaper's legal counsel. Question after question was put to him, and he only had answers to a few of them. Thus, concluded the attorney as he presented his case to the jury, "Mr. Ford is ignorant."

Ford's own lawyer then took to the stand and began asking some more questions.

"Mr. Ford, when you need to know the answer to any of the previous questions, what do you do?"

Ford's reply teaches us one of the secrets to true entrepreneurial success. It is a commonsense secret that is the opposite of what we're taught as specialist employees.

"When I need to know about finance, I call in my finance manager and ask him all the questions I need to have answered. The same goes for sales, production, or any other subject," Ford replied. "I pick up my phone and speak to my sales manager, production manager, or whoever the expert is on the subject I need an answer to."

In other words, the smartest leaders in the world employ specialists who are smarter than they are.

Henry Ford knew what every strong leader knows: Being a strong leader, rather than a manager, is about becoming a generalist, not a specialist.

A specialist is easily replaceable. A specialist is taught to follow. A specialist ends up working for a living, rather than living a life.

Generalists, on the other hand, think for themselves. They are great leaders, they take on the risks, and reap the rewards, and more importantly, they collect long-term income from the work they do today.

In the truest sense of the word generalists are leaders. They live by the ideal that it's better to have 1 percent of one hundred people's efforts than 100 percent of their own. Becoming a generalist is the first major task anyone considering venturing into business for himself must tackle. It's the single biggest mind-set change all employees who want to start their own businesses must make. Being the best at your trade, your profession, or your job in no way means you'll succeed in the world of entrepreneurial business.

OK, so now you're a generalist, having taken the decision to delegate—to let go and to trust your team members to get on and do what they have to do. What now?

Well, you will have put in place some very important building blocks upon which your new, exciting, and very positive business environment will be built.

As mentioned previously, these moves will be reflected in your company's culture, but perhaps more importantly, it will set a precedent as far as influencing each individual team member's belief systems.

What exactly does this mean? Well, you know that in most businesses, people follow the example of their most senior executives. To put this another way, the boss sets the example. The workers look to the boss for what goes and what doesn't. You've probably also heard the saying, "When in Rome do as the Romans do." It's the same in any business. What's good for the goose is good for the gander, to coin another phrase.

People's belief systems are something that is fundamental to them. They help shape their very identity. I like to explain this by means of my iceberg analogy.

**The Identity Iceberg**

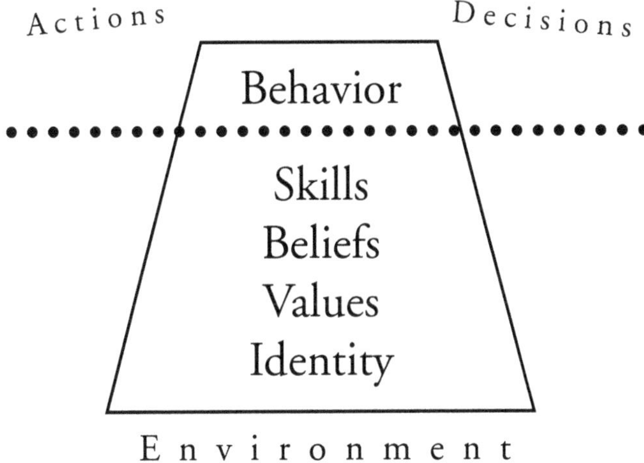


When you see people, be it at work or at home, the only part of them that you can view is that external part that is characterized by their actions and decisions. This is that visible part they show to the world, much in the same way as we can only see the tip of an iceberg—you know, the part that sticks out of the water.

The bulk of the iceberg is, of course, invisible to the rest of the world, because it is under water. With people it is much the same. They only expose to the rest of the world a small portion of their entire being. The rest is invisible. However, this invisible portion has a huge influence on that which is visible.

Their level of skills, for instance, is invisible to us yet it manifests itself in what they are able to do. Now this is something that is very visible. If you were to spot a person walking down the road, you would never know that she might be a talented artist, until you happened to see one of her works. Or you might one day see her in action. Then, and only then, would you realize that she was indeed very talented, because it would suddenly become obvious through her actions—through her behavior.

Below the level of skills there is another invisible level called beliefs. Here reside a person's inner beliefs about everything. And these deep-seated beliefs profoundly influence everything that person thinks or does.

There are two more invisible levels and these are values and identity. Can you see how people's skills, beliefs, and values affect their very identity? If you can, then you will also realize that, by changing your level of skills, beliefs, and values, you can actually change your very identity.

Isn't that interesting?

And of course, by changing your identity—by becoming the person you want to become—your behavior would change.

Now, remember that this iceberg floats around in an environment. It doesn't exist in a vacuum. This environment influences, and is influenced by, the iceberg. See, if it were to float in a warm ocean, it would begin to melt, but if the temperature of the sea were very cold, it would grow by freezing more. It could also influence the temperature of the sea around it by lowering the surrounding temperature.

In business it's just the same. You certainly can influence your business environment—both physically and attitudinally—and this will in turn influence your team members by helping to change their beliefs about work in general and your business in particular. By helping to show them, through your own example, that your business (and their working environment) is the ideal place to spend most of their waking hours, you will be doing much to affect their enthusiasm, their productivity and efficiency, and your business as a consequence. You will be helping them to realize, in the most direct and dramatic fashion, that they must choose to become *victors* and not *victims*. You will be helping them to assume full responsibility for their own lives. I'll discuss *victors* and *victims* in more detail later on.

Don't be afraid of giving your team members responsibility for their jobs. This means you must let them take over the reins. Let them run their work area or job as they see fit—and always within the boundaries of your playing field, of course. Remember the Loose/Tight culture we discussed previously? This is where it comes into play. Learn to let go and to trust in your team members; you did hire them to do the job, after all. And you did select them individually from all the others that applied, didn't you? That means you selected the best people available. And if you nurture them correctly, it should come as no surprise to you that they are very much better than you are in that particular job. You should, in any event, be regarding yourself as a generalist and not a specialist. Your team members are the specialists—not you—so let them get on with it.

Of course, expecting them to assume full responsibility for their jobs is a two-edged sword. You must also give them accountability. They deserve to reap the rewards of their actions and decisions. So let them. This is why I always recommend implementing a reward system based on the achievement of Key Performance Indicators.

What we have been looking at here are positive ways in which you can nurture or develop a positive environment for your business. These are the proactive things you can do to influence the work or office environment. But there are others.

There are things that your team can do that will also affect their environment. Things like the way they interact with each other. Of course, this should be covered in your Points of Culture. In this way, your business can become a positive, happy, and vibrant place where your people will enjoy being. By taking a collective decision not to tolerate gossip, to avoid situations in which office bullies can thrive, or by making a point to stamp out all forms of discrimination, be it along race, gender, age, or physical lines, the work environment will be transformed into the kind of place that will become the talk of the town and the envy of all.

Now that all the mental or attitudinal factors are in place for the creation of a winning environment, there's one more thing you need to do. You need to put in place a safety release valve because we are, after all, dealing with human beings.

Because your team can make or break your business, you need to set up mechanisms to foster team spirit and a culture that will promote the values as set out in your Mission Statement. One way to do this is to establish weekly "WIFLE" sessions (*W*hat *I* *F*eel *L*ike *E*xpressing), in which team members have uninterrupted time to speak their thoughts without fear of recrimination. This is really a very powerful safety release valve that works very well indeed. I've introduced it to thousands of businesses all over the world.

You might also want to improve your physical environment. If you don't have the budget, don't worry. It needn't cost the earth. Just adding fresh flowers to your reception area and indoor plants to the various workplaces can make a world of difference. Of course, you could do things a little more elaborately if your budget allows. You could, for instance, repaint your building inside and out and upgrade the furniture. Adding music or hanging pictures on the walls can also transform your work environment. There's no doubt about it, people really do perform better when they feel better.

You might also want to consider consulting a feng shui expert or buying a book about it. This is a whole specialized area of its own, and I make sure my work places are set out according to feng shui principles because it really does make a difference.

What is feng shui? It's a Chinese system that seeks to harmonize our relationship with our work or home environment. The words literally means "wind" and "water."

Your team members' performance will change for the better if they feel more comfortable in their jobs. We've just talked about making their environment more comfortable from a physical point of view, but you can make it better for them too by better equipping them from a knowledge point of view as well. By this I mean you can offer them some form of ongoing training to ensure that their skills improve. You see, your business will grow only if your people do, so design an ongoing training system to ensure they acquire new knowledge all the time.

But most of all look after those who work for you. Make them feel part of the family. Here are some things you could consider:

- Hold team skill-based sessions.
- Develop a Social Club.
- Subscribe to educational newsletters and industry magazines and make them available to all your people. This will keep them abreast of developments and make them feel well informed.
- Take care of new people from the moment they join your business by having in place an induction training program.
- Be sure to run regular team-building training programs.
- Build career planning within the company.
- Set company and individual team member goals.
- Run Time Management Training.
- Make sure you have a full set of positional "How To" manuals and encourage your people to refer to them often. If you need assistance writing them, refer to my book *Instant Systems.*
- Whenever you are dealing with people, the potential for conflict exists, so develop a system to resolve conflict.
- Develop, and publicize, your company's Rules of the Game—this will help minimize the potential for conflict within the workplace.
- Put in place a system that addresses redundancies in a fair and equitable manner.
- Complete a consistent recruitment system.
- Develop contingency staffing plans.
- Hold regular team meetings.
- Develop a system for recognition and remuneration.

- Use Behavioral, Personality, and Communication Analysis with all team members—your *Action* Business Coach can assist you with this.

Your team can make or break your business. Develop the right environment and nurture your people through the development of effective, farsighted staffing plans and systems. Remember, you can train your people and lose a few of them to other companies along the way, or you can neglect to train them and lose your business. Which would you prefer?

Part 5

# Put Systems in Place

Systems—this has to be one of the most misunderstood areas of business today. I find this rather strange, because it's the one area of business that is easy to implement, and one that will make your life, and that of your team members, so much easier. And it also happens to be something that will make your business run smoothly, efficiently, and more profitably.

I'm big on systems for another very important reason; they allow your business to work *without* you.

That's right—they will allow you to live your dreams, to do the things you want to do, and to spend your time pursuing other, more lucrative goals like increasing your wealth.

Let that sink in for a moment.

I know it seems to be 180 degrees away from what you've been taught in the past. Think about it; why build a job for yourself when you can build an income stream that keeps on growing whether you're there or not? Remember this one simple fact: the only reason you would ever start a business is to sell it at some point in time. Your business is your product; it's what you're building, and it's where you're ultimately going to make your profit when you sell it.

Very few people ever make a fortune running their businesses, but a lot of people make a fortune selling them.

Look at Bill Gates, for instance. Sure, he's made a lot of money selling software, but he became the richest man in the world by selling shares in his business, Microsoft.

Are you too involved in your business? Could you pick up the phone in the morning and say to whoever answered, "You guys look after things; I'm taking three months off." If you are like the vast majority of business owners out there, you would very definitely answer "*no.*"

Why? Because your business wouldn't have the systems in place to allow it to function effortlessly without you.

Let's look at it from another perspective. Perhaps you don't trust your team members to get on and do the job themselves. Perhaps you just can't let go of running "your baby." Perhaps no one there can *do* the job as well as you can.

If this sounds familiar, ask yourself this: why did you buy or start your business in the first place? Think hard now. And be honest with yourself. Did you not just buy yourself a job?

Understand that this is *not* what owning a business is all about. If you continue working *in* it and not *on* it, then your business will never grow and prosper, and it will not reach its full potential.

It's for this very reason that you have to get yourself out of the day-to-day routine of running the business. Stop working from nine till five, doing the work *of* your business. It's like the carpenters that don't run their businesses. Instead, they spend all day using a hammer and nails, working *in* their businesses.

Imagine that when you started your business, you built it in your mind first, and then you drew a picture on paper of what it would be like when it was finished. That's right, you've got to finish a business at some stage and have it ready for sale.

As an example, imagine buying this book after I'd only slapped together an outline of each chapter. Imagine buying it before I finished writing it. How much would you pay for it? Only a fraction of its full price, I'll bet. The same happens in business. People try to sell a business that hasn't been finished, so they're really only selling a *job.* Of course, in this case they'd only ever get a fraction of the price for it too.

When you've got the finished picture firmly in your mind, you then go to work creating that business. That means working *on* the business, rather than just working *in* it.

In fact, you're designing the business so it will run whether you're there or not. Then you've got choices, and choice to me equates to freedom. You can keep the business, or you can sell it. You can work in the business or you can spend your time more creatively.

Now take a moment and imagine a business in which you didn't have to work. Would the business WORK? I mean, would it function properly? Would all the systems and people integrate to achieve the result you want, the result your customers want? *Of course it would.*

Almost every business owner I've ever met works so hard *(too hard)* for this exact reason. Their business doesn't work—they do. Everything about the business is in their heads, and they're the only ones who can do anything, so they're trapped. Imagine my example of this book and how hard I'd have to work if this knowledge were only in my head.

Most owners are like this because they don't trust anyone else to do the job. For some reason they believe that no one can do the job as well as they can. They have to be in control.

All great leaders are good at delegating, so start off-loading some of your tasks *now*!

By the way, once you've given your team members the job to do, let them do it. Don't jump in to save them; that way they'll never learn how to get the job done. All they will learn is that you're the only one who can fix things, so you always will. Remember, sometimes you have to let them fall off the bike to learn how to stay on.

What you will be aiming at doing is systemizing your business so that it's run by systems and not people. That way it will run smoothly and according to plan all the time. It will be consistent. By that I mean it will run the same way day in and day out. The level of service your team provides will be consistent, the product range you manufacture will be consistent, and the businesses level of efficiency will be consistent.

Yes, but what will your people do, you ask? They will run the systems.

That way, when something goes wrong (and it inevitably will because nothing stands still forever), all they have to do is fix or amend the system.

So how do you go about systemizing your business?

## Involve Your Entire Team

It is extremely important to explain to all team members exactly what you'll be doing, why, and what the expected outcome will be *before* you begin documenting or observing what they do. The last thing you want is for them to jump to the wrong conclusion—the grapevine will spring into action and your intentions could backfire badly. Explain that it's not a witch-hunt, that you're not looking for excuses to do away with them or their jobs, and that you're not aiming to consolidate various positions and making some of them redundant.

You really do need to ensure you get all team member on side for an exercise like this because if you do, they can be of enormous assistance, and if you don't, you could end up with a massive problem on your hands. So consult widely and honestly. Involve them in every step of the exercise. Communicate genuinely and hide nothing. Let them know what your intended outcome is—making the business run smoother, more profitably and efficiently—with major benefits for them, their workload, and their level of job satisfaction.

Get this aspect right and it can turn into a major team-building exercise with huge benefits as far as team morale is concerned. If you involve all your team members from the very beginning, they will buy in and take ownership of the exercise. Your job will become very much easier, the end result will be much more effective, and the final outcome will exceed your wildest expectations.

## Document What Each Team Member Does

The next thing you need to understand, and document, is exactly what each team member does on a daily, weekly, and monthly basis.

This is a fairly detailed task and one that could take a fair amount of time to complete. But it's absolutely necessary that you don't cut corners, take shortcuts, or leave things out. The object here is to gain a clear and accurate picture of what happens in your organization. This will give you accurate data from which to produce your system as well as provide information to allow you to streamline the operation, making each position more efficient.

There are various methods you could use to achieve this. They include the following:

- Interview the team members.
- Ask the team members to write a detailed report of what they do.
- Observe the team members.
- Video the team members.
- Record on audiotape details of what the team members do.

Once you have produced a detailed description of what each end every team member does, tidy it up and edit the copy so that it reads well. Then get the team members concerned to review what you have written in order to give you their approval or suggest corrections so that the end result is an accurate reflection of what happens in their areas of responsibility *at that time.*

Remember, don't jump ahead here and start changing what they do because you have uncovered more efficient or cost-effective ways of doing things through this task audit. That's not the purpose. You see, you are interested, at this stage, in getting a detailed map of how things run in your business *at the moment.*

And you can't guess or assume anything here. Everything will be thoroughly tested and measured to ensure it works as intended later on. But if it doesn't, then at least you have a safety measure up your sleeve.

Run through this exercise with everyone in that functional area or department, and then do the same for the next functional area, and then the next until you have worked your way through your entire organization. Collate the documents together and the end result will be a detailed snapshot of what goes on in your organization, workwise. You could think of it as a comprehensive operations manual. File it in a folder and put it to one side for the moment.

It is important to bear in mind that what you are aiming for here is something quite different than a set of job descriptions or Key Performance Indicators. Resist the temptation to take a shortcut here by simply using people's job descriptions. You see, what a person *actually* does in a job and what they are *supposed* to do are usually quite different. Furthermore, we are aiming at compiling a detailed account of what *happens* every day, week, or month and not what *tasks* need to be looked after. Get the difference?

This is important because when it comes to writing the systems, you will be concerned with finding out what is working and what isn't in every job in your business. You will be looking for better, more efficient, and cost-effective ways of conducting your business, with benefits in everything from customer satisfaction to team satisfaction, and from an increase in profit to a more efficient business operation. Job descriptions can't help you achieve this.

Once you have a complete and detailed description of what your team members do on a daily, weekly, and monthly basis, your next task will be to test and measure what they are doing to see if it is producing the required results.

Now's the time to compare these activity schedules with their respective Job Descriptions and Key Performance Indicators (KPIs). The aim here is not to catch people out or to go about pushing them to work harder in a sneaky way; it's about finding better ways of doing things.

The Japanese have a great word for this. They call it *Kaizen,* and it means "constant and never-ending improvement." Think of your quest for improvement as a circle; it has no beginning and no end. It is a never-ending quest. You should just keep getting better all the time. When you have reached your goal as far as improvement is concerned, then raise the bar a little and try again. When you reach that level, raise it again and improve some more.

Test each job one at a time. Start by comparing what is actually done with the KPIs. Are the KPIs being achieved? Are they all being achieved on time, or only some of them? What are the reasons for this? Can steps be put in place to correct this?

Once you have ascertained how each job scored, you need to now involve your team members. Get them to do the following:

- List their top 10 time-consuming tasks.
- List their top 10 stressful tasks.
- List their top 10 productivity-related tasks.
- List their top 10 tasks that bring them the most happiness.

Now, how can you accommodate the above four lists in their daily, weekly, or monthly routines? Can you streamline, adapt, amend, correct, or include something new here? Ask your team members to think about any bottlenecks they are aware of. Get them to list the three that they believe are causing the greatest problems to customers or your bottom line. You'd be surprised what they actually know about your operation—they do, after all, work closely with it day-in and day-out. Work at eliminating these problems one at a time. Then have a look at making absolutely sure the team members' 40 points are taken into account. You see, not only will you be taking their concerns on board, you'll be seen as doing something positive to address some of the major job-related issues facing them. Having satisfied or content team members means your business will operate most efficiently and cost-effectively. There will be a real sense of purpose and pride, and your customers will pick this.

Now it's time to rewrite, with the assistance of each team member, the daily, weekly, and monthly task descriptions. Alter the job descriptions and KPIs accordingly. Monitor how they are performing and coping for a month, then test and measure the work descriptions against the KPIs once more. You should see a huge difference in performance levels, job satisfaction, and results.

## Writing the Systems Manuals

So how do you go about actually writing the systems manual? It's not as daunting as you'd imagine. Here are some considerations:

- Start with the workflow descriptions.
- Use bullet points and concise headings.
- Start with the first, most important, or regular task.
- Itemize each action that is needed to handle or complete each function, and write briefly what needs to be done.
- Mention what the desired outcome is, and what happens next.
- Remember to mention what happens if things go wrong or if another action is called for.

Now that you have a basic set of systems in place and you're reasonably happy that they are working, it's time to concentrate on writing or developing systems that affect the business as a whole—ones that will put your business well and truly on the fast track to operating smoothly, efficiently, and like clockwork all day long.

We are now not going to be concentrating on writing systems not at the job level, but higher up at the corporate level. These will be company systems that will focus on how the business operates in its entirety.

When viewing any business from a corporate perspective, there are four key areas that override or encompass each and every other system that you may have in place. You see, there are some that will be common across the board, so rather than duplicating them over and over again for all your different functional areas, these systems are grouped together under the corporate portfolio.

So what are these four key areas of the business? They are:

1. People and Education
2. Delivery and Distribution
3. Testing and Measuring
4. Systems and Technology

By concentrating on writing systems for these broad areas, you'll be putting in place ways to make your business work more efficiently and effectively. To find out about these in more detail, read my book *Instant Systems.*

Part 6

# Recruiting Team Members

Once you have good systems in place to run your business, the next thing you need to concentrate on is finding the right people to run the systems. Of course, I'm taking a very simplistic view here, because most readers will probably already have people working for them. You can't just fire everyone and start over again with a clean slate. That's simply not possible.

Existing team members can, of course, be molded and developed according to your overall plans and ambitions. This is what this book is all about. But the time will come when you need to recruit new team members.

The aim of this part is to outline how I go about it. I will use real examples taken straight from my own recruitment system at **ActionCOACH.**

When you hire new team members, you have the advantage of being able to impress upon them, right at the outset, what you expect of them, what the rules of the game are, and how they must go about performing their duties. You see, they will be coming into your organization fresh; they will be totally unaware of any situation that might have existed previously, before you set about changing your company to meet new objectives or goals.

Experience with many businesses I've worked with shows that, when new systems or smarter ways of going about the way they do things are instituted, many existing team members leave. They become uncomfortable and don't like the idea of either having to learn new ways or having to move outside their comfort zones.

Recruiting new team members becomes necessary.

And this isn't always such a bad thing, because these new team members will accept the situation they find as being normal. They are therefore usually very much easier to work with.

A great team is one of the best assets a business owner or operator can invest in. The way in which organizations find or recruit team members is important, as excellent people can only enhance your business.

So how should you go about finding excellent people?

The *Action* Recruitment Process is broken down into four sections, and I'll cover them in turn. This system is designed to be flexible enough to work over and over again. It is also designed to take the stress and hassle out of employing team members. The sections are as follows:

## Advertising

Before you begin drafting your classified advertisement, there are some important issues you first need to get clear on.

You need to spend some time thinking about the type of people you are trying to attract. Who is it you want to employ? What skills and characteristics do you want them to have? What other attributes would you like them to have? Can you form a mental picture of such people in your mind?

You see, most employers focus only on the skills needed to do the job. Other attributes like personality traits, passion for that type of job, or what they can contribute to the workplace simply don't come into it. This is a shame because these "heart" and "spirit" aspects of any job applicant are, to my mind, the most important. Skills can always be learned, improved upon, or acquired, but passion, personality, and heart are the things that will give any team that winning edge.

Once you've decided what types of people you want to attract, how do you go about writing an ad that will make them not only take notice, but actually want to call you?

Most people wrongly believe that good ads have to be funny, well written, or visually dramatic. The truth is that the very best ads work because of the strategy behind them.

Here's a good analogy. If you've prepared a delicious meal and your dinner guests are hungry, they won't care what kind of plates you use. Put another way, if your message appeals to the people you're writing to, it barely matters how you present it.

Of course, there are things that you can do to make your ad clearer, more direct, and more interesting, but these are definitely secondary concerns. If your strategy is wrong, the best penmanship combined with the best graphic design in the world won't save you.

Imagine trying to encourage teenagers to invest $400 a week for their retirement. On the surface, it sounds like a reasonable idea, but realistically, you'd be lucky to get a single interested adolescent. The strategy is completely wrong. First, you're going after the wrong groups of people, and second, the amount you're asking for probably exceeds their weekly income.

That's an extreme example, but a good one to highlight the problem with most ads—they say the wrong things to the wrong people.

By now I hope you realize that the most important aspect about writing any ad is to target it properly. This is why you must have a very good idea of the type of person you can see filling your vacant position. The most important component of any ad is the target—the person the ad is aimed at.

The only things you really need to consider when writing copy for an ad are:

- How to target your ad to the people you are trying to reach?
- What will make them respond?
- What is the best way to communicate this to them through your copy?

When it comes to writing the copy, here are some hints to keep in mind:

- Be specific.
- Be exciting.
- Focus on the benefits of the job.
- Write as you speak.
- Write in the present tense.

- Keep it simple.
- Follow the AIDA formula—*A*ttention, *I*nterest, *D*esire, and *A*ction. It must attract their attention, then make them interested enough to read further and build their desire enough for them to take action and to apply.
- Be credible.
- Include a good headline that's easy to understand—longer ones work better than short ones.
- The headline should be a question, as this is the most successful type.
- Include an element of curiosity.
- Qualify the reader.
- Use words your reader can relate to.
- Get to the point, as soon as possible.
- Keep your sentences short.
- Include a call to Action.
- Include contact details.

You can read more about writing successful ads in my book *Instant Advertising.*

Here are some advertisement templates that I have used in the past. Tailor them to your organization and then simply place them with your preferred newspaper or magazine.

## If you're the bookkeeper we're looking for... You'll be...

Friendly, charming, enthusiastic, and conscientious ... You'd have high standards and be described as courteous, mature, and a relaxed team player ...

You'll be responsible for 4 major roles with **ActionCOACH** at our Milton based office—daily banking, accounts receivable, accounts payable, as well as the completion of daily reports ...

You'll need to be well presented, trustworthy, punctual, and love smiling. You'll be eager to take this opportunity to learn, grow, and achieve well above average results and remuneration.

You'll apply the skills you already have in accounting practices and accounting programs. These skills are desired though not 100% essential.

**If you believe this is you, be ready to show me why when you call me before 5 pm this Friday on 07 3367 1555 ... in fact just call me NOW ...**

## If you're the Junior Team Member we're looking for ... You'll be ...

Friendly, charming, enthusiastic, and conscientious ... You'd be described as being courteous, having high standards, mature, and yet a relaxed team player ...

You'll be responsible for 4 major roles within **ActionCOACH** at our office based in Milton. These are Data Entry, answering calls from our clients and prospective clients, getting orders and marketing letters in the mail,and keeping communication flowing in the office.

You'll need to be well presented, love smiling, trustworthy, and punctual. You'll be keen to take this opportunity to learn, grow, and achieve well above average results and remuneration.

You'll apply the skills you already have in data entry, Windows-based programs, and have worked previously in a similar role.

**If you believe this is you, be ready to show me why when you call me before 5 pm this Thursday on 07 3367 1555 ... in fact just call me NOW ...**

**Are YOU ready to SELL for Australia's leading Marketing Consulting and Training company?**

Brad Sugars

If you're the sales person we're looking for, you'll be driven, self-motivated, successful, great at selling over the phone, and wanting to earn at least $75,000 a year.

You'll be pushed, asked to achieve great results, taught about business marketing, and eventually trained to become a business consultant. You'll sell to dozens of business people each and every week. You'll accept only the best performance from yourself and your team, and you'll be ready to take a long-term challenge to create success in both your life, and with Brad Sugars' Company, **ActionCOACH**. You'll be inspired, passionate, motivated, and above all ready to learn, *sell*, and push yourself to achieve more than you ever thought possible.

**If this ad describes you, then be ready to sell yourself and call us before 5 pm Wednesday on 07 3367 1555**

## Callbacks

These days any job advertisement is likely to result in an avalanche of replies, so you really do need a system to cope when the phone starts ringing. By the way, I prefer respondents to call in rather than to mail in their applications like so many companies want them to do. This is because anyone can pay to have a great looking resume produced, yet this will tell you absolutely nothing about the real person behind the application.

You see, what you need to be concentrating on here is the "body" and "soul" aspects of your applicants, not their level of skill and past experience. This is totally irrelevant, as they are applying to work at a different company with different attributes, expectations, and ways of doing things. You want to find the best possible person for the job, not just any person who can do the work. You are ultimately looking for that one person who wants the job more than anything else in the whole world. You are looking for someone who is passionate about the job.

Because of the large number of people who are sure to apply, you should be aiming to run a deselection process rather than a selection one. You see, you will want to weed out all the average performers—those who just want a job—and you'll want *them* to do it for you. That's right—the average performers will weed themselves out of contention for you. And this process starts with their initial callback.

You have two choices regarding how to handle the callback: you can take the calls personally (or have one of your team do it for you) or you can set up an answering machine and get the applicants to leave a message.

Let's deal with the telephone response first.

## Telephone Response

It's vitally important that you make use of a telephone script, because there are certain important pieces of information you must capture. Writing a good script is easy. Just remember the cardinal rule: keep to the point and don't ramble on too long.

Read through the script in a relaxed manner. Don't make it obvious that you are reading, because that will make you sound unnatural and unprofessional. Have a pen handy and jot down answers to the relevant questions in the spaces provided on the bottom of your script. That way you won't have to rely on your memory when the time comes for the face-to-face meeting. It will also help you to jot down a first impression rating, which will be useful if you receive a huge response.

Remember, you can tell a lot from a telephone conversation. Tune in so you can form an initial impression about the applicants' personalities. Are they bubbly, dull, or enthusiastic? You will even be able to tell whether they are smiling when talking to you. How friendly were they? Are they self-assured and confident? How articulate are they? These are all important clues to how organized their thought patterns are. Logical thinkers tend to be logical speakers too. You will also be able to ascertain how easily the applicant is able to relate to a complete stranger—you.

Are you beginning to see that this is the type of information that is so important to have before making a final decision? Can you appreciate that none of this is available on a resume?

So, how does a real script look? To give you an idea, this is the one I use at **ActionCOACH.**

**Telephone Response**

Good Morning. Thanks for calling **ActionCOACH.** This is .............

Great. Let me just start by getting down your contact details.

NAME ... as you can see from the advertisement, we do things a little differently here. And, because of the number of people we have applying for this position, and to make sure you get a chance to hear about our company from the Chairman, what we're doing is meeting everybody who applies at the ..................... ................. on .............................. the .................; that's ................. ........................... evening, from 6:00 pm till 10:00 pm. There, you'll learn all about our company and the position you're applying for.

But NAME, before I give you the rest of the details, let me just ask, what was it about the ad that made you decide this position was for you?

Have you got a pen handy so I can give you the details for Wednesday evening?

Great, NAME, I'll be putting some more information about us in the mail for you today. Can I ask you to bring it along with you together with a copy of your resume for us to keep on .................... evening? I look forward to speaking with you then.

First Impression ........../10

Name .........................................................

Address .......................................................

..................................................................

[ ] Checked on Interview

Phone ...............................

Is this person Male ... Female ...

What was it about our ad that made you decide this position was for you?

..........................................................................................

..........................................................................................

..........................................................................................

..........................................................................................

Comments

..........................................................................................

..........................................................................................

D I S C V A K

Was this person smiling ...Yes/No Final Impression ........../10

Your Name :.................... Time .........am/pm Date ......./......../.......

**Answering Machine Response**

In many instances, taking calls personally may not be appropriate. You could, for instance, be anticipating a huge response that would simply inundate your entire team. Some ads attract well over a hundred replies; would you be able to cope?

In cases like these, setting up an answering machine on a dedicated phone line is the answer.

Once again, you would make use of a script when recording your message. I find the best is to modify and adapt the one you'd use for the telephone response.

What you are essentially aiming at here is to get the respondents to tell you something about themselves as well as leaving their contact details so you can get back to them if you feel they show potential.

I always ask my respondents to tell me what their three strongest attributes are, why they feel they are suited to the position, and what their biggest success to date has been. You'd be surprised at how many people find this so intimidating that they drop out then and there. They deselect themselves, which is the aim of this exercise.

You see, when they call in, the last thing they expect is to have to answer some very probing and profound questions. And they aren't given much time to think about their responses. They have to think as they go along. This certainly tests their motivation and passion and gives a very good indication of their character.

I listen to the responses first thing each morning, jotting down on the response form the relevant answers. Once I have these, I am then in a good position to make a decision about who to progress to the next stage—the interview.

This is what my answering machine response sheet looks like:

**Answering Machine Response**

First Impression ........../10

Name ..........................................................

Address ........................................................

.................................................................

Phone ................................

Is this person Male ... Female ...

What are your three strongest attributes?

.............................................................................................

.............................................................................................

.............................................................................................

.............................................................................................

Why are you suited to this position?

.................................................................................................

.................................................................................................

.................................................................................................

.................................................................................................

What is your biggest success?

.................................................................................................

.................................................................................................

.................................................................................................

.................................................................................................

D I S C V A K

Was this person smiling ...Yes/No Final Impression .........../10

Should this person be invited to the interview? Yes/No

Why?

.................................................................................................

.................................................................................................

Called by:................. Time ..........am/pm ... Date ......../......../........

## The Interview Process

Once your have received all your responses, you will be in a position to review them according to the overall classification you gave each one initially. It's now time to develop a short list (ideally the top four or six) based on the classification rating.

The next thing to do is to set a date for the interview process. I find that to conserve time, it is better to hold a group interview with all your team members (depending on the size of the team) and the short-listed applicants attending. Contact each short-listed person and invite him to attend the interview. You could do this by phone or by letter. Here are examples of both:

Date:

Name:

Address:

Hi, NAME and Welcome...

This letter is our way of introducing you to the team at **ActionCOACH.**

As you've probably already noticed we do things a little differently than most people in business and that's because we operate on a few totally different beliefs about what's going to work should really mean.

We believe that:

- Going to work every day should be a joy.
- You should love to come to work early and stay late.
- You should work as hard on creating a better *you* as you do in your job.
- Making mistakes is great...as long as *you* take responsibility and learn from them.
- You'll always enjoy being a part of the team...if the team wins, we all win.

And so on.

You'll be able to learn a bit more about our culture and what we strive to achieve by reading our Corporate Vision and Culture Statements following this letter. You'll also get to learn a little more about what we'd expect from you as a team member if you were to join us by reading about going the extra mile.

As you'll already know, you've been selected to join us at the Parkroyal Hotel on the corner of Albert and Alice Streets in the city on XXX day the XXXX from XXX till XXX. We may run a little over if we need to learn a little more about you.

I know this seems different, using the Boardroom in a nice hotel, but our time is really valuable, so we like to meet with you and all of the other people we've selected to come to our interviews at the same time.

In that time, we'll tell you all about our company, the position you'll be applying for, and answer all of your questions. Please be sure to dress as if you were coming to work and have a copy of your resume that we can keep to go over.

Look forward to meeting you then...

All the best.

Brad Sugars

Chairman

P.S. If you have any questions before the meeting please call us on

07 3368 2525.

**Script for Inviting Potential Team Members to 1st Interview Session**

Good Morning/Afternoon, *(applicant's name)* this is *(your name)* calling from **ActionCOACH;** you left a message to apply for a position with us ....

*(Applicant's Name)*, I was just calling to invite you to join us in our interview process. As you might have realized we do things a little differently here; would you be available next *(Day)* night at the *(Venue)* from six till ten in the evening?

**NO**...Well unfortunately that's the only time we can do this first stage, so unless you can find some way to make it at that time, we'll have to say thanks for applying and leave it at that.

**YES**...Great, have you got a pen handy so I can give you the details?

We'll be holding the interview from six o'clock right through until ten o'clock next *(Day)* evening at the *(Venue)*, it's at *(Address)*.

You'll need to bring your resume with you and dress just as if you were coming to work.

*(Applicant's Name)*, can I just check the address we have for you is correct? We have...*(Applicant's Address)*

Great, I look forward to seeing you at 6 o'clock next *(Day)*...Good-bye.

The goal for the evening is to introduce applicants to your organization, letting them know what their role will be as well as how this role fits into the organization as a whole. But perhaps most importantly, you'll be aiming to determine whether the applicants best suit your company's needs.

The reason I ask my entire team to attend is because it is they, after all, who will have to live and work with the person who is ultimately selected. It is for this reason that each member of my team has an equal say in whom we choose.

Most applicants find this process very daunting (even intimidating), as they are used to having one-on-one interviews. However, this is the intention because it is, after all, a deselection process. We never go out of our way to make it daunting; it's just that it's the last thing they expect. We always make them feel at ease, and we take the opportunity to show them that we are indeed a very different company than what they might ever have come across before. This is the best way to give them a glimpse of our culture and working environment, and it works extremely well for us. You see, the main aim here is to find a perfect match; we are trying to fit a round peg into a round hole. We are seeking compatibility.

The evening is conducted according to a set format. Here's an example of how the evening will unfold:

**New Team Four-Hour Format**

6.00 Greet and welcome, making sure everyone listed is in attendance.

6.10 Brad to lead the group in Vision, Mission, and Culture of Company and where it's going. Also to discuss "Going the Extra Mile."

7.00 Team members to tell the group of their experiences in the workforce and the difference at *Action*.

7.35 Brad to describe the current situation at *Action* and its history to date.

7.50 Brad to give job description.

7.55 Brad to give format for rest of evening and send to 15-minute break.

8.00 Break and chat.

8.15 Potential team members to introduce themselves to the rest of the group.

8.40 All to fill in questionnaire.

8.55 DISC Evaluation.

9.10 VAK Evaluation.

9.25 Brad to ask group questions.

10.00 Finish and let know who will be contacted tomorrow...check phone numbers.

### Things to Look For in a Resume

Make notes on the interview sheet

1. Consistently good grades in math and English.
2. Did the applicant participate in any team activities?
3. Teachers' written comments.
4. Presentation and effort.
5. Things it *leaves out.*

### Questions to Ask the Group

Each person must answer each question in turn.
Make notes on the interview sheet.

1. What sort of jobs have you been applying for? Why?
2. What are you looking for in a job? Why?
3. What do you want to achieve in life?
4. How do you see *Action* helping you get there?
5. What one thing made you apply for this position?
6. What do you think the job is all about?

We also rely on a checklist to help with the preparation and smooth running of the interview session. It looks like this:

### *Action's* Pre-interview Checklist

**Venue:**

[ ] Venue booked and confirmed

[ ] Seating arranged

[ ] Projectors booked

[ ] Signs made for directions

[ ] Notepads and pens for each seating

**Refreshments:**

[ ] Lemon water arranged

[ ] Mints on each table

[ ] Handouts

[ ] Going the Extra Mile copied

[ ] Handouts copied

[ ] Interview sheets distributed

**Applicants:**

[ ] Inform them of Venue, Date, Time

[ ] Confirm attendance the day before

[ ] What to bring, eg. Resume/CV

[ ] Name tags

When everyone is seated, we hand around copies of our Vision, Mission, and Culture Statements, as these will be thoroughly discussed once proceedings get underway. Team members are given an Interview Evaluation Form, which looks like this:

## *Interview*

**Name : -** ................................................ **1st Impression** ........../10

**Presentation** ..........................................................................
..........................................................................................
..........................................................................................
..........................................................................................
..........................................................................................

**Resume** ..........................................................................
..........................................................................................
..........................................................................................
..........................................................................................
..........................................................................................

**Question Time** ..........................................................................
..........................................................................................
..........................................................................................
..........................................................................................
..........................................................................................

| | 0 | 1 | 2 | 3 | 4 | 5 | 6 | 7 | 8 | 9 | 10 |
|---|---|---|---|---|---|---|---|---|---|---|---|
| Responsiveness | | | | | | | | | | | |
| Attentiveness | | | | | | | | | | | |
| Positivity | | | | | | | | | | | |
| Happiness | | | | | | | | | | | |
| Neatness | | | | | | | | | | | |
| Commitment | | | | | | | | | | | |
| Common Sense | | | | | | | | | | | |
| Practical Ability | | | | | | | | | | | |
| Honesty | | | | | | | | | | | |

**General Comments** ..........................................................................
..........................................................................................

**This Person's Strengths** ..........................................................................
..........................................................................................
..........................................................................................

**Their Weaknesses** ..........................................................................
..........................................................................................
..........................................................................................

**Final Impression** ........../10 **Conclusion** .......... **Yes / No**

 TRS010

When the presentations are at an end, application forms are handed out to the applicants, and they are asked to complete them and hand them back to a team member before leaving. We also tell them that a decision regarding a second, one-on-one, interview will be arranged for the two most suitable candidates, and that everyone will be phoned and advised of the outcome the following day.

This is what the Application Form looks like:

**Your Application to Join the Team at ActionCOACH**

Your Name........................................................................................

Your Address....................................................................................

Your Phone Number..........................................................................

Your Sex............ Male / Female...........................................................

When you're asked at the end of this evening, please take the time to complete these next few questions.

What did you hear this evening that touched you?

..........................................................................................................

..........................................................................................................

..........................................................................................................

..........................................................................................................

What have you done in the past that you believe you could add value to the story I've told you?

..........................................................................................................

..........................................................................................................

..........................................................................................................

..........................................................................................................

What one impossible hurdle have you had to overcome in your life that has caused you to believe that you're a "stayer?"

..........................................................................................................................

..........................................................................................................................

..........................................................................................................................

..........................................................................................................................

What is it about the position we described that appeals to you?

..........................................................................................................................

..........................................................................................................................

..........................................................................................................................

..........................................................................................................................

Any other comments:

..........................................................................................................................

..........................................................................................................................

..........................................................................................................................

..........................................................................................................................

**STOP**...Wait until this question is mentioned before you answer it...After everything you've seen and heard, do you want to go further in this interview process..................Yes / No...

## Decision Making and Follow-Up

After meeting with the applicants and reading through their questionnaires and resumes, the decision about who to choose should be easy to make. Of course, you should base your decision on the feedback you get from your team members.

They will need to take into account the applicants' performance as well as any information received from verbal references (previous employers if necessary) and written references that might have been attached to resumes.

Here's an example of a script to use when obtaining a verbal reference:

### Getting a Verbal (Phone) Reference

*The object of this is to get a brief history of a person's work to enable us to ask some pertinent questions at the interview, and to find out how the person has worked in the past.*

Applicant's Name ________________________________

Keep the team member's application open in front of you, 2nd page and complete the following:

Name of Supervisor for reference ____________________

Phone Number ____________

1. Dial the number.
2. Smile warmly as soon as the phone is answered.
3. Say, "Good Morning/Afternoon.

   "This is ____________________ (your name)

   "from _____________________ (your organization)

   "May I speak to ______________________ (the supervisor listed above)?"
4. Before continuing, confirm that you are speaking to the person named.
5. Say, "Your name has been given by ____________________ (Applicant's name) for a verbal reference. He/she has applied to work with us. May I ask you a few questions about _______________ (Applicant's Name)?"

The questions are:

a) What was the approximate period of employment?

b) And the duties?

c) And the reason for leaving?

d) Was ______________ (Applicant's name) honest with money?

e) And was ______________________ (Applicant's name) accurate with money?

f) What system do you have to assess honesty and accuracy with money?

g) And was _____________ (Applicant's name) always punctual?

h) And reliable?

i) Did ______________________ (Applicant's name) have any sick days? If so, how much notice in advance of the rostered-on time was given?

j) And did ___________________ (Applicant's name) take any days off as holidays?

k) Was ______________________ (Applicant's name) ever late to work, or ever went home early?

l) Would you re-employ ________________________ (Applicant's name) again, if he/she applied for the same position now? And why?

m) How did you rank _____________________ (Applicant's name) as a member of your team (top, average, bottom)?

n) And what was the reason for being at this level?

Say "Great. Thanks very much for your time. That answers all my questions about (Applicant's name). Bye for now."

Your Name___________________Date: ______ Time: _______

Be careful not to base your final decisions on the level of skills your applicants have alone—you need to take into account personality factors—what I call heart and soul factors—as well as their general level of enthusiasm. Try and guage whether each applicant will fit in with the rest of your team. Will there be friction with existing team members because of different DISC personality profiles? Will personalities clash? What will the applicant add to your business?

When you have chosen your new team members, notify them of your choice as soon as possible to make sure they are still available. Then arrange a meeting before they join your team to discuss salary details as well as various housekeeping matters like working hours, the dress code, and office etiquette. This meeting can be conducted over the phone if they can't come in for whatever reason.

It's equally important to notify all the unsuccessful applicants, as they will want to know where they stand so they can continue with their job search. They may also have another job offer, in which case they'd want to be in a position to act quickly so as not to lose that one while waiting to hear from you first.

You can notify them either by phone or letter. Here's an example of a phone script you could use:

## Unlucky Applicants Phone Script

Thanks for applying for our position...and thanks for coming along last night...it was a little different, wasn't it?

We all really enjoyed the evening and I'd just like to wish you all the best in your future job hunting. We just felt that the position wasn't exactly what you're looking for...

Although we do feel that you have a lot of strong attributes and we're sure you'll find something very soon that's better suited to you.

Thanks and all the best for the future...

Part 7

# Getting the Beliefs Right

People's innermost beliefs are the fundamental cognitive contents of their brain that they hold to be true. Or to put it another way, they are the psychological results of perception, learning, and reasoning. What we are talking about here is knowledge in its purest form.

If you "know" something to be true, it will form part of your belief system. You will simply "believe" it to be so.

When we begin examining our beliefs, we are dealing with the things at the very core of our existence. You see, we base our entire value system on our beliefs. And collectively, we base our whole society on these shared values. Freedom of speech, freedom of association, and freedom of religion are just some basic cornerstones of our whole way of life. They are fundamental values that have been enshrined because of what we believe in as a nation.

Not all people believe in the same fundamental principles. That's why we have different nations and different "societies" on this planet. We are who we are because of our beliefs, our values, and the skills we have. These three attributes combine to give us our identity.

It should become apparent to you now that if you want to change your behavior, you really need to reconsider or alter your beliefs first. Doing this is the surest way of achieving lasting and meaningful change. You see, once you've changed your beliefs, you basically change who you are. And a "new" you will act or behave in a different way to the "old" you.

Make sense?

It all has to do with your mind, because that's the domain of your belief system. It's where your thoughts reside.

I'm now going to spend some time discussing the brain and how it works, because once you have a general understanding of this, you will find it very much easier to work with different people as you strive to develop your dream team.

What I'm aiming at here is making certain that you adopt the right attitude towards your life, your existence, and your business. What I am talking about lies at the very core of positive thinking. It's fundamental to everything we do if we want to be successful.

Still not quite with me? Then ask yourself this: Are you one of those who say the glass is half empty? Or do you say it's half full?

It's more than simply a question of being either a pessimist or an optimist. These are nothing more than the outward manifestations of something much deeper—something more fundamental and profound. You need to get straight to the core of your very being, and then to prepare it so it will accept the challenges that lie ahead in such a way that living the life you *really* want to lead will simply happen. I'm talking here about really turning dreams into reality through the power of your mind.

So where do you start?

Right here. And right now.

## Are You a Victor or a Victim?

To start with, we need to exercise the brain. It's time to get imaginative for a while.

Think of the world as consisting of two distinct groups of people. Think of these two groups as those who see the glass half full and those who see it half empty. Now think of them as being separated from each other by a horizontal line. One group lives above the line while the other lives below it.

I call these groups *victors* and *victims.*

Everyone is either a *victor* or a *victim.* There are no in-betweens. They play the game (it can be any game; it can be the game of life, business, sports, or parenthood) below the line or above it.

| | |
|---|---|
| **Ownership**<br>**Accountable**<br>**Responsible** | **VICTOR** |
| **Blame**<br>**Excuses**<br>**Denial** | **VICTIM** |

The first thing those who play below the line do is to *blame* other people. They come up with *excuses.* They *deny* what they are doing or what is going on. They blame the economy for their poor performance in business, they use their difficult boss as an excuse for their lack of progress, or they deny their marriage breakup had anything to do with them. If this sounds like people you know, it means they are playing the role of *victims.*

Those who play above the line say, "OK, let's take *ownership* of our situation. Let's take *responsibility* for our actions. Let's be *accountable.*" If you play above the line, you're basically taking responsibility for your life. You're saying you're accountable for your results. You're saying you're not a *victim;* you're a *victor.* You're saying you're in charge of your life.

You might be surprised to learn that 95 percent of people live their lives below the line.

Most people just stumble along, blaming others for their lot in life. They go through life in denial. They've always got a good excuse why they haven't been able to succeed at whatever it is they're doing.

If those who live below the line want to succeed, they've got to shift into the zone above the line. That may take a quantum shift in their belief patterns. It may also require them to challenge the way they view life. But they have to do *whatever it takes* if they want to take control of their lives; once they assume responsibility, they'll be amazed at how they suddenly start making progress towards achieving the things that they previously only dreamed of—and so can *you*!

To fail is human. And we are all human. Often the difference between a *victor* and a *victim* is not the number of failures we make, but how we have chosen to deal with them. *Victors* take control of their lives; *victims* let life control them.

Remember, perfection leads to pain and standing still. Strive for excellence instead. Be a *victor* and enjoy the financial abundance your winning attitude will bring.

Success is the constant process of moving toward your goals no matter what obstacles life throws in your way. Play above the line, take control of your future, and make it all it can be.

## Left Brain, Right Brain, and the Learning Process

Now that we've covered the basic way you need to apply your mind to ensure you take responsibility for your actions, we need to spend some time understanding what the brain is and how we can harness it so we can achieve our goals. You see, what we've covered so far is understanding how we can *apply* our minds so we view our existence positively and from an above-the-line vantage point.

What we are now going to do is to gain an understanding of *how* we can apply our brainpower—our minds—so we can instantly, and without effort, harness its power to automatically turn dreams into reality. Not possible? Then read on.

Let's start by understanding, in very brief terms, what our brain is and how it works.

The brain is made up of three main parts: the hindbrain, the midbrain, and the forebrain. They sit one behind the other along the brain stem. The complete brain makes up about 2 percent of our body mass and 15 percent of total body metabolism at rest. Even at rest the brain is functioning, pumping electrically charged ions across its membrane to produce electrical signals that are given off by the nerves.

Most of us don't allow both hemispheres of our brain to function simultaneously, but we all have the ability to. And why do we need to use both sides of the brain? Easy. Numbers, words, and logic are left brain factors. But you need the right side—the creative—to see how to put deals together, to see what others don't. All it takes is practice.

For most of us, when the left and right brains work simultaneously, we learn and make decisions rapidly. However, generally prior to learning something new, we need to experience some level of confusion. Now confusion in itself isn't a bad thing, because it makes your brain work in a higher state—it has to work out what is going on in addition to running all its usual tasks and processes.

The challenge is that when most people experience confusion, they just say, "I don't know." If you're ever going to be successful, you have to learn that confusion means that it's time to ask a new question—a better question; then you'll move forward. Let's pretend that we are pondering the question, "How powerful is my brain?" Most people would simply throw up their hands and say they don't know. They would become confused and not even know where to start looking for the answer. But what if their immediate response was to ask another question? A better question. What if they then asked, "What is meant by the word 'brain'?" They could then make progress by responding, "In this case, let's assume we are dealing only with the physical brain. Now, what are the parts called, how much space do they occupy, and what are their functions?" They immediately have more information to go on. When those have been answered and they can't pursue the question any further, instead of experiencing more confusion, they should pose another question. "Has anyone else been able to answer such a question before?" This would open up the possibility of finding out what other researchers have found. They could then ask the question, "Who has studied the brain in the past?" Do you see what is happening here? The more you ask, the more you move toward finding an answer to your initial question.

But let's go back a little at this point. What we do know is that in our first five years of life we learn the most we'll ever learn. We learn everything from walking and talking to discovering as much about our immediate environment as we can. We learn to recognize people, how to react to certain situations, and what is good and what is not. From then, until about the age of 16, we settle into thought and behavioural patterns that will stay with us for the rest of our lives. We develop habits that can become very difficult, but not impossible, to change later on.

But, change habits we must. If you're going to change your beliefs, you have to learn different things, think a different way, and therefore do different things.

It's impossible to change beliefs without learning new things.

So, how do we learn new things?

Just because you didn't succeed at something doesn't mean you are a failure. You see, the only real failure in life is the failure to try.

Remember back to when you learned to ride a bike? You probably had someone stand behind you, holding the seat to balance you as you started to pedal. You probably wobbled all the way down the driveway at first, safe in the knowledge that someone was supporting you. Then, after a few attempts, you turned around to ask a question, only to find she wasn't there. She was standing up at the top of the driveway watching you with a big smile on her face.

Then you promptly lost confidence and fell over.

Did you give up there and then? No, of course not. You climbed back onto your bike and tried again, only this time you made sure someone ran behind you with her reassuring hand firmly holding the saddle. However, the time came when she let go and you were able to stay upright on your own. Now think harder. Can you remember exactly when she let go of the saddle? Probably not. All you may remember is rejoicing in the fact that you could ride. What an exhilarating feeling that was! From that moment on, you could ride unaided. And it was a moment you'd never forget.

Learning is all about taking some sort of *Action*. You have to do something. It's not a passive process. I can give you education through this book, or at a seminar, but you still have to learn by doing.

Understand this: Give a person a fish and you'll feed him for a day. Teach that person to fish and you'll feed him for a lifetime.

I believe the most dangerous two words in the English language are the words "*I know.*"

If somebody tells you something, and you say, "I know," your brain goes into filter mode. You see, because of the amount of information it is being constantly bombarded with, it tries to avoid overload and filters out what it already knows or has. It discards surplus information. The problem is, generally, it's what you "know" that really isn't correct, and this stops you from succeeding.

At one time, people really "knew" the sun revolved around the earth. They were absolutely convinced this was a "fact," and the rest of their knowledge and reasoning was based on this assumption. Until Galileo (1564–1642) appeared on the scene, that is. This forward thinker became well known for thinking outside the box. In 1630, he published his views about the orbital motion of the earth around the sun. It changed the world forever.

I would suggest you banish the phrase "*I know*" from your vocabulary and replace it with either, "As I understand just now," or "What I believe right now." This creates two improvements: it makes your brain function at a higher level, and if at a later time you discover you were not quite right, you won't go into self-destruct mode—you'll need only to change a belief or increase your understanding of the situation.

Let's now consider the words "*knowledge*" and "*wisdom.*" What's the difference between them?

Having knowledge means being able to relate something you've just heard to something you already understand. Having wisdom means understanding both how and when to apply that knowledge.

Understand this: You can have all the knowledge in the world, but if you don't do anything with it, you end up with nothing at all. You need to apply it; you need to take *Action* to achieve results.

For you to truly learn how to change your beliefs, you have to add to what you know, and in most cases, totally edit (that is remove) some of your old thinking and replace it with entirely new thoughts.

It's all about attitude. It's about what you're thinking. If you're broke, it's only because you're broke in your mind. If you're wealthy, you have to be wealthy in your mind first. Some people just don't believe this, but if you do, it'll make a *huge* difference.

You have to understand that your mind is a very powerful thing and it'll give you everything you want out of life. The challenge for most people is that they just don't believe this. They don't understand how to use their mental faculties to make things happen for them.

So, why is this so important? Simple. Most of the deals I do, anyone could have done. It's just that they thought poor, so they didn't see the rich deals.

Ever heard the saying that positive thought leads to positive action? Well, it's true. Rich thoughts lead to rich actions, or, put bluntly, you need to *think* rich to *be* rich.

Why do you first need to think rich? Why not just concentrate on becoming rich?

A very good question—and it all has to do with the way the brain works. This is where the Reticular Activating System comes in. Be sure to read this section well, as it could be the most powerful information you'll ever learn.

## The Reticular Activating System

One of the main distinguishing features of the brain, I think, is that it has to do with the equally mysterious subject of consciousness. What actually is consciousness? I know it seems like a simple question—even a stupid one—but think about it for a while and you'll suddenly find that you get into all sorts of difficulties. For instance, we know it's essentially a very private matter. You "know" you are conscious, because you just are. You can think, reason, plan things, do and feel things, and experience emotion. But you can do all these things when asleep—when you are not conscious. When you wake up in the morning, you "know" you were dreaming and that what you dreamed about was not real, yet it may have felt very much so at the time. But here's where things get even more complicated. How do you "know" that other people are conscious? You may believe they are, but it's very difficult to prove. This is what philosophers call "the problem of other minds."

So what is the definition of consciousness? It can be defined as "an alert cognitive state in which you are aware of yourself and your situation." That's what the dictionary says, but is it necessarily true? Philosophically it can be thought of as the subjective—the I that seems to have some existence over and above the body. But this leads us once again down that subjective path that isn't very helpful, because what is subjective to me may not be to you.

Neuroscientists have learned a great deal about the anatomy and physiology of the brain—they know about its different parts, what they do, and how they interact with each other—but they know very little about the mind. They are puzzling over the relationship between the physiology of the brain and consciousness. They are in fact finding it very difficult to tie the mind to the brain. Some question whether the two exist independently while others wonder if it is the result of some as yet unknown force.

We do know that ideas are things of the mind. But can they exist independently of the mind? I really don't know. But what I do know from my research and experience is that we can control our ideas, which in turn can affect or control our very existence.

Let me explain.

Remember back to the last time you bought a car? All of a sudden you noticed there were hundreds of that very same model on the road. Here's another example: try right now to *not* picture in your mind a pink elephant with wings. Your brain has the amazing power to create or find whatever you focus on. This is the job of the Reticular Activating System, which can be thought of as your personal compass.

Your Reticular Activating System will find proof that the earth is flat if you want it to. In fact, it'll find proof that November is a slow month for your business if that's what you want. In other words, attention determines direction.

Here's another example: if you were to ask a person how his day's been, and he answered, "Not bad," what would be his benchmark on life? BAD, and today's not that. Your brain is an amazing tool and it'll find whatever you ask it to find, so you'd better be sure to ask for very positive things.

Remember to ask for the things you want, and *not* to push away what you don't want.

Every day your business meets your true expectations. In other words, if you believe you've got to work hard to make money, then that will always be your reality. If you believe you can never get good people to work for you, that'll be your reality. Remember, you generally make true what you believe to be so. We even have a term for this because it's so well accepted. It's called a "self-fulfilling prophecy." Isn't that interesting?

What I want you to be aware of at this stage is that there is a thing called a Reticular Activating System in your brain and it's something very powerful that you can use to make your dreams come true. Here's a great example of how this works.

Steve Leach, one of *Action's* coaches, tells the story of how he stumbled across a new client.

It happened quite out of the blue one day a couple of years back.

"We had been experiencing a water leakage problem at home," Steve explains. "There was moisture coming through our bathroom wall that was causing the paint to flake. My wife had mentioned it a couple of times, so it was on my 'subconscious' to-do list."

"That weekend, I almost had an accident with a van that touted 'waterproofing solutions' for builders. By the time I'd found a pen and paper to write the number down, he was gone. I made a mental note to fix our water problem and look in the yellow pages for a supplier, because it did strike me as coincidental at the time. The next day, I was driving down the coast to run a training session and noticed a different 'water solutions' truck driving beside me. I hastily took down the number to call later, now regarding this as something of a 'karmically significant' event, as Deepak Chopra would call it."

"After training I was driving back home and again found myself driving next to the very same truck. I'm sure the driver noticed my repeated stares and wondered if I'd been shadowing him all day."

"The next day at the office I received a phone call. It was from a company wondering if I could help it build its business. I asked what business the company was in. The answer—waterproofing solutions! It was a completely different company from the two I had encountered in previous days. 'I've been waiting for your call all day,' I responded. 'What kept you so long?' I signed them up and began working with them soon thereafter. And what a lucrative contract that turned out to be, added of course to the fact that I got my bathroom fixed for free."

Wasn't this just a case of good luck? Not at all; you see, his Reticular Activating System had locked into water solutions, so he was tuned in to receiving signals connected with it. He became alert to the possibility that presented itself. Good luck is, he says, nothing more than opportunity meeting preparedness.

## You Are What You Think

If you accept the proposition that your ideas shape your reality, then if you were able to change what you think about, you could change your reality. This is powerful stuff. Just think about it for a minute.

By thinking, you have the power to change your very reality.

If this were the case, why then are most people quite content to go through life unhappy with the situations they find themselves in?

## Factors That Stop You from Changing Your Reality

What is it that prevents 95 percent of people (those who live their lives below the line) from living the lives they want to live?

If you could understand the reasons, do you think you'd be able to do something about it? Do you think you'd have a good chance of ensuring that you don't belong to that 95 percent when it comes time for you to make the crucial decisions in life? You bet!

If I were to tell you that there are eight primary factors that stop you from living the reality of your dreams, do you think you could do something about it?

Good. Here then are those eight factors:

### 1. Habit

We do what we do because of well-ingrained habits. A habit is something we do automatically. But habits can be changed. It only takes 21 days to instill a new habit; that's all. Just concentrate on doing something in a different manner for 21 days and it will become a habit. Or concentrate on not doing something for

21 days and you'll lose the habit. Remember, a breakthrough usually follows a breakwith, a breakapart, a breakup, or a breakdown. Sometimes we need one of these things to happen before we can make a break-through in changing a habit. Always replace a habit with one that is more beneficial to you. This is what I like to call a RICHual.

### 2. Tradition

What you've always done in the past won't solve the problems of the future. Past thoughts and actions may have been effective then, but they'll probably not be effective in meeting the demands of the future. If you want things to change in your life, *you* have to change. It's that simple. Remember, if you choose not to change, you will keep getting the same results as you're currently getting.

### 3. Peer pressure

How many times have you made a decision based on what other people thought? On what your family or friends thought? Understand this: If you allow other people to make your decisions, you'll get the results that 95 percent of the population gets. Either change the people you associate with, or remember this: *What other people think of me is none of my business.*

### 4. Lack of knowledge

Keep learning every day, because if you think education is expensive, try *ignorance.* Learning is a four-step process. Once you see it this way, it becomes easier. Here the four steps are:

1. *Unconscious incompetence:* This is when you don't even know that you don't know something. We've all been there. How would you know you need to learn about a particular aspect of investing for instance, if you weren't aware it existed?
2. *Conscious incompetence:* As you experience things, you become aware you're lacking in knowledge in a certain field. At least you now have the choice to do something about it.
3. *Conscious competence:* Now you can do it, but you have to be totally focused on it. Remember the first time you drove a car or rode a bike?

4. *Unconscious competence:* Once you have mastered something, you can do it without thinking, like driving a car. Once you're experienced, you can listen to the radio or engage in conversation while driving. You're able to coordinate the gears, clutch, and steering without consciously giving it any thought.

When I first learned the four steps of learning, I believed I had to go back three steps to "conscious incompetence" to learn a new way of doing something. I found this extremely difficult, as my natural instinct was to go forward, not backward. Now I understand the stairs just keep going, and I have to continue to learn even though I believe I may understand all there is to learn. There is so much out there that we don't even know that we don't know.

**5. Fear**

If you allow fear to stop you from striving to live the life you want, you are leading a secondhand life. What I mean by this is that you are consciously making a decision that results in your lifestyle and enjoyment being limited, because you are allowing a negative emotion to control your life. You may not be in control of your destiny, but you are in charge of the decisions you make on your journey. By understanding what fear really is, you'll see how you have been deceived. Fear stands for "*false expectations appearing real.*" Fear is nothing more than an illusion. Illusions are easily dealt with. However, one of the results of fear is stress.

Remember this: *If you have no influence over it, you shouldn't concern yourself with it.* We all have concerns—with our health, work, international affairs, the environment, the economy, or today's youth. Some of these things we can do something about and some we can't. If we spend most of our effort worrying about things we can't influence, we will tend to lead reactive lives.

However, there will be some things that fall within what I call our "Circles of Concern" that we can influence. Perhaps our work and our health are areas where we do have some influence. These then fall within our Circle of Influence. If we were to focus on the things we can influence, we would lead a more proactive life. The trick is to slowly expand our Circle of Influence to include some of the things that were previously only of concern to us. If we can do this, we will grow.

So, how can we cope with stress? If you're feeling rather stressed, ask yourself two questions: on a scale of one to ten, how life threatening is it? And, again on a scale of 1 to 10, am I doing the best I can? If the answer to the first is below 5, then forget about it. If it ranks higher, then obviously you'd do whatever you need to do to ensure you remain alive long enough to deal with the second question. If the answer to the second question is below 5, then again you shouldn't waste any more time worrying about it. If the answer is above 5, then just keep doing the best you can at that time. You'll realize that, until now, you have always coped, so why wouldn't you in the future? Just get stuck in and do what you have to do. Worrying gets you nowhere. And neither does stress.

## 6. Apathy

Apathy can be a very strong force in stopping you from changing your reality. To understand apathy, let's consider what it is that motivates us. There are three main motivators: fear, desire and greed. Fear is a very popular motivator. People may have a fear of being unable to finance their retirement, a fear of failure, or even a fear of death. Of course, we all know that greed motivates many, but that's a negative motivator because it often blinds you to the real issues or risks. Greed is really only fear in disguise, a fear of being without. We all desire things, and if we desire them enough, we can become focused on achieving them. We become stirred into *action.*

To overcome apathy, you need to change your behavior or thought processes. You need to make a conscious decision to change your reality. Here's my formula for change:

$$\mathbf{D \times V + F > R}$$

This means *Dissatisfaction,* multiplied by *Vision,* plus the *First Steps* have to be greater than your *Resistance.*

If you want to change, you need to increase your level of dissatisfaction or you need someone to help you increase your vision. You also need someone to help you take your first steps, or to reduce your resistance.

Some people teach that you have to hit rock bottom before you are able to change. That's stupidity. I'd much rather have less resistance to change because then things don't have to get too bad before I make the decision. You see, to change what you're doing doesn't mean you first have to stop what you're doing.

Most people give something a go, then, if it doesn't work, they simply give up and focus their attention on reinventing the wheel. They try to develop a system from scratch, instead of fine-tuning their original attempt and trying again. They should rather keep going by trying a different approach until it works.

To change something in your own life, you don't need to be totally dissatisfied. You do need a vision, some guidance, and, most importantly, you need to overcome your resistance to change. You need to change your thought processes.

## 7. Pride

Some people would rather *look* rich than *be* rich. Consider these scenarios. A person bought his first house for $100,000 and started repaying his loan at $600 a month. After three years he sold for $120,000, paid off a few debts, and bought a bigger house for $150,000 with a loan repayment of $900 a month. Then three years later, he again wanted to upgrade, so he sold for $180,000, paid off his car, and bought another house for $200,000. The loan repayments went up to $1200 a month. Three years later, he was tempted with an offer on his house of $250,000, so he sold, thinking he had done extremely well, having basically upgraded from a $100,000 house to one worth $250,000 in nine years. In reality, he still owed about $200,000 to the bank, but he did have $50,000 in cash.

Sound familiar? Yes, I'm sure it does. We've all done it.

But if that same person had focused on wealth creation right from the start, from the time he bought his first house, he would have hung on to the house and swallowed his pride, increasing his payments to $900 a month after three years, then $1200 a month after six. After nine years he would have paid the house off, and it would probably have doubled in value. So he would be worth at least $200,000, without owing anything.

In the first scenario, our imaginary friend would be *looking* rich with his $250,000 house, but the person in the second scenario would *be* rich with a $200,000 house that he owes nothing on, and $50,000 in the bank.

## 8. Identity

How do you see yourself? Do you think of yourself as being *rich:* an investor, wealthy, smart, and successful? This is most important.

You see, your greatest asset is your mind.

You need to think about the characteristics that identify you as a person. They could include integrity, passion, honor, creativity, open-mindedness, decisiveness, discipline, risk-taking ability, adaptability, motivation, focus, confidence, persistence, knowledge, and being proactive.

Can this become your identity? Why not? There's no reason at all why it shouldn't. You see, it's a simple matter of making your mind up that it will. Just be clear about the results you want to achieve. You might have to change a few things first, like worrying about what other people think about you. The decision's yours. It can be done.

Let me show you how:

## Choosing a New Identity

Right now, jot down all the things that you think you are. Then, take a clean sheet of paper and write down all the things that you need to do to give yourself the new identity that you want. That's right—draw up an Identity Profile of the person that you want to become.

Remember this: the two most powerful words in the English language, when put together, are "I am."

How will this look? What sort of personality traits will you need for your new identity? What kind of identity do you want? Let's look at the last question first.

Decide what identity you want to assume. This is the personal identity that will help you assume a new reality. Your desired identity might be one of the following:

- A successful team member.
- A business tycoon.
- A well-respected and successful business leader and family man.
- A powerful politician.
- An innovative community figure.
- A successful writer.

The list is endless. It all depends on what type of reality you want to create for yourself, but I hope you get the idea.

Now let's consider the personality traits that you might need to help you assume your new identity. They could include the following:

- I am creative.
- I am competent.
- I am knowledgeable.
- I am motivated.
- I am always learning.
- I am committed.
- I am decisive.
- I am organized.
- I am forward thinking.
- I am positive.
- I am a good negotiator.
- I am healthy.
- I am honest.
- I am a great investor.
- I am a rich thinker.

Once you have compiled your list, revisit it regularly to remind yourself who you want to become. And be prepared for people to get in the way and distract you. If this happens, move away. Only associate with positive, like-minded people. The fact of the matter is that unless you focus on achieving this, you'll slide back into the person that you were. That means you'll achieve the results you were achieving previously. You need to constantly grow towards the person you want to become. It's much the same for a tree—it either grows or it dies.

The important thing to realize is that it's not what changes in your reality or physical environment that's going to determine whether you become successful or not. It's not changes in the economy or your financial situation but the changes that take place inside your head that will make all the difference. Here I'm referring to things like your level of knowledge and your thought processes. I like to put it this way: It's what you're saying to yourself about yourself when you're by yourself that will affect you most. This is the only thing that, at the end of the day, is going to determine how rich you become. Have the right attitude, and you'll create the right life for yourself. It's really as simple as that. Anyone can do it—it's just a matter of whether you choose to or not.

Understand that everyone wants to *have* things; some people understand that they need to *do* something in order to *have* what they want. Very few people understand that they need to *be* the people who can *do* what is required, to *have* whatever they need in life.

In other words you are a human being, *not* a human doing or a human having; so work on *you.* Be the best you that you can be.

## Building Your New Reality

Once you have decided on the characteristics of your new identity, it's time to focus on visualizing your new reality. You need to have a picture firmly in your mind of how your new reality will look.

This is important because what you concentrate on in your mind has a tendency to expand. Your mind is no different from any other muscle in your body. If you exercise it regularly, it will develop. It will grow. Thoughts—the seeds of your mind—will grow to become your reality if you exercise them.

To begin with, what you need to do is to create a *rich* mind. You must create a mind rich in thoughts, rich in attitude, and rich in self-esteem. Remember, you need to *think* rich before you can *be* rich. You have to think that you're a good leader before you can be a good leader.

The next thing you need to do is to expand the picture in your mind of yourself and your new reality. You must concentrate on this step now, even though you haven't yet decided on exactly what your new reality will look like. Confused? Let me explain.

Have a closer look at your vision right now. If you don't have a vision, don't worry. Another name for it is your dream. Now, that is something you will almost certainly have. You see, we all have dreams. We all dream about what we'd like to be, how we'd like to live, and how nice it would be to be successful and wealthy.

Think about your vision for a moment. Picture it in your mind's eye. See it in vivid color. Luxuriate in its rich imagery. Let your mind run riot.

Now expand that vision.

That's right—make it even more lavish. Dream bigger. Think in terms of *and,* not *or*. Dream of having a new house *and* a new car, not a new house or a new car. You must exercise your mind to accept the *and* option instead of defaulting to the *or* option. Why settle for second best? Dream of having it all. After all, some people do, so why shouldn't you? It's there and it's available—it's there for the taking.

Aim for the stars; that way if you don't quite achieve it first time round, at least you'll reach the moon.

Once you've created your new vision—an expansive new vision—it's time to plant the seeds that will make your vision a reality. This is the fun part. Follow the three simple steps and you can't go wrong.

1. *Create your list of affirmations.* Use the two most powerful words in the English language—"I *am*." Use very positive terminology, and make sure to use the present tense. They will most probably be the same as those you wrote down when redefining your new identity. They could include the following:

    - I am creative.
    - I am competent.
    - I am knowledgeable.

- I am motivated.
- I am always learning.
- I am committed.
- I am decisive.
- I am organized.
- I am forward thinking.
- I am positive.
- I am a good negotiator.
- I am healthy.
- I am honest.
- I am a great investor.
- I am a rich thinker.

Write this list down, preferably in bold type and a large font size, and pin it up in a prominent place where you will see it every single day from now on. It could be pinned up on a notice board in your office, on your mirror in the bathroom, or alongside your computer screen on your desk. Now read it out loud every single day. You could do this first thing in the morning, at lunchtime, or last thing at night; the exact time doesn't really matter. What is important, though, is that you do it. You see, what you are doing here is fixing these characteristics in your Reticular Activating System. They are becoming part of the workings of your mind.

2. *Create a dream chart.* Now it's time again to have some fun. Get ahold of a stack of magazines—say two dozen. It doesn't matter what kind of magazines they are, as long as they contain lots of words and color pictures. Page through the magazines one by one, paying particular attention to the pictures. What you are looking for are pictures or words that signify your idea of an ideal existence. It could be a great ocean yacht, a monster flat screen television set, or a magnificent house with a simply stunning ocean

view. It could also be lazy days on a sunny beach somewhere, nightlife in Paris, or an ocean cruise. Cut them out and glue them onto a large sheet of cardboard. What you'll be creating here is a collage of pictures that, when viewed together, will present a snapshot of what your ideal reality looks like. This should take a few hours to complete. When you've done that to your satisfaction, hang this picture up in a prominent place—somewhere you're sure to see it every morning. It could be on the wall alongside the mirror in your bedroom, on the wall in your study or office, or in your kitchen.

3. **Visualize your reality**. This is the most important step. Invest 20 minutes each morning visualizing your new reality. This is solitary time; make sure you're not interrupted at all. Turn off your mobile phone, television set, or radio. Don't allow interruptions from your partner or children. Put the dog or cat out and get comfortable. Then close your eyes and focus on everything you've pictured in your new reality. Think deeply and succinctly. Imagine yourself there living the life you aspire to. *Think* yourself there. Let your mind wonder; let it enjoy your new reality. Think of the fun you'll have entertaining your family and friends on board that yacht. Think of the fun you can have in Paris. And how comfortable life will be in your new seaside mansion. Soak up the atmosphere and relish the thought of being able to live the life of your dreams. Understand that what you're doing is nothing more than planting the seeds of your new reality. Plant the seeds every morning. Make it part of your daily routine.

It's important to realize that what you are doing here is essentially to create a new you. You are in the process now of becoming a different you. When you have become someone different, you will do things differently and you will achieve different results. This is true because you can only do what you are, so if you want to do different things, you first need to change who you are.

Here's another important thing to bear in mind: Since your *subconscious* mind deals only with thoughts, it cannot determine the difference between dreams and reality. So feed the dreams as often as you can. This way your Reticular Activating System will lock onto them and things will start to happen for you. You will find yourself drifting strongly towards your desired reality.

If you create a bigger picture of the lifestyle or reality you want, and then use the three-step technique to impress this picture upon your subconscious mind, you will be amazed at how this new reality will begin to materialize. As you change who you are, you'll change what you do, which in turn will change what you have.

Your new reality will unfold right before your eyes.

And it will do so effortlessly. That's right; you will not have to fight, struggle, or work hard for it to happen. This is a simple truth because that's the way of nature and the universe. Nature always takes the easy route. The laws of nature that govern everything in the universe are not convoluted, complicated, or complex; they are simple and straightforward. Just think of some for yourself and you'll see what I mean. Take for example, the law that says every action has an equal and opposite reaction. Or the law of gravity.

If you understand this, you'll understand why I maintain that it's only natural for us to live a life of abundance. We should all have everything we desire—and more. There is, after all, more than enough of everything to go around. I believe this so passionately that it is the vision statement of my major business, **ActionCOACH.**

You'll also appreciate why I say the key to success is laziness. Many regard this as a little controversial, but I'd rather have 1 percent of 100 peoples' income than 100 percent of my own. If you've ever thought you'll succeed if you just work a little harder, put in some extra time, or just do more of what you're doing right now, then it's time you lifted your head and took a look around you.

Millions of people work hard, but they're not really getting anywhere, are they?

The aim of the game isn't to work harder; it's to create better results with less effort—finding ways of achieving more with less. In other words, to continually *leverage* your time, your efforts, your money, and your knowledge.

If you're paid an hourly wage, you'll never earn more than the number of hours you work, but if you and your business are set up so you're paid whether you work or not, then you've truly understood one of the key principles of success, and that's leverage to have more. I believe so strongly in the principle of leverage that I've even created a board game, called "*Leverage,*" to teach people how to apply it to their businesses in a fun way.

Leverage is simply the ability to do more with less. You see, employees earn money and business owners make money. Now take that one step further; entrepreneurs and investors collect money.

I have devoted my life to teaching business owners how to create an income stream that flows whether they work or not.

## Lead by Example

Once you have successfully changed your own beliefs about yourself and have changed into the person you want to be, others will notice. They will see changes taking place right before their very eyes because your actions, behavior, and decisions will be different.

And so too will be the results you achieve.

You will begin to influence the members of your team because success is infectious. They will want to emulate your performance for two simple reasons: They will be inspired by what they see, and they will perceive new standards of performance in place. Understand that this is a very positive environment you will be creating. It will be one focused on success and achieving results for everyone. Your team members will begin to feel the results in a very real way because they will be achieving more with less—and having fun while they do it. This is, after all, one of the ultimate aims of being in business, isn't it?

Their successes will be yours, and yours will be theirs. This is what strong leadership is all about.

Part 8

# Synergy

What is synergy? Why is it so important in business today and how can you ensure your team has it?

Synergy can be defined as "the working together of two things to produce a result that is greater than the sum of the individual things." Put simply, it's like saying 1 + 1 = 4.

Think about it for a moment and you will realize that this is exactly how it works. Let me give you a good example of an actual case.

It involves Greg Albert, one of my Business Coaches, and his client, DK Design Kitchens in Harbord, New South Wales. I'll bring them both in shortly and let them talk for themselves.

## The Challenge

If you've ever lived on a busy road, you'll know that after a while you become oblivious to all the noise. You become immune to the very things that other people find most irritating, frustrating, and off-putting. You'll find that you begin focusing on other factors, things like convenience, atmosphere, and lifestyle as a means of justifying, in your own mind, at any rate, why it is you've chosen to live there.

You'll be looking for reasons to stay there, whereas others would be looking for reasons why not to stay there. They'll cite factors such as noise, inconvenience with parking, and lack of privacy as good reasons for finding a quieter place to live.

Familiar with the scenario? Good. Then you'll understand that the same can happen in business.

Just because the business owner is engrossed in the job doesn't mean other members of the family are. The spouse could be more than frustrated by the long hours worked and lack of social activity, whereas the owner might see things quite differently. And not as objectively.

Take the case of DK Design Kitchens, for example. The business had grown steadily since its inception, but this was more a result of doing things as they came along than good planning—of luck and lots of hard work.

Both Jakob Gamborg and Preben Lemming had been in the industry before they joined forces. Jakob had been in sales and design and Preben in manufacturing. They both felt they could do better than the companies they worked for. You know the story—"I thought I worked for an idiot *before* I went into business for myself." And if you've read Michael Gerber's book *The E-Myth Revisited*, you'll know what I mean when I say Jakob and Preben were typical technicians. Their only concern in those early days was survival and making enough money to cover expenses.

DK Design Kitchens grew into a design, sales, and manufacturing company located on the northern beaches of Sydney, with a mission to become the North Shore's most prestigious joinery business.

Preben is in charge of production while Jakob is in charge of sales and design. Preben's wife Pernille looks after administration and accounts.

Everything seemed to be running very nicely—or was it?

## Pernille's Story

We first came to hear about **ActionCOACH** when we were offered a free business diagnostic through a direct mail letter. We took up the offer and found out how much more **ActionCOACH** could do for us, although we still weren't sure anyone from outside could help our company.

At the time of meeting Greg Albert from **ActionCOACH,** the company had grown to 15 employees. Our sales were OK—though not great—but workflow and speed in the factory were in disarray. It is safe to say our team was not happy, and we had a lot of "reworks" and some unhappy customers.

When Jakob first met Greg, he said, "This guy can't tell me anything about selling and sales; I have been doing this for 12 years and know what to do."

However, I knew something had to change; we were working long hours, not making much profit and had a lot of fires to put out.

Preben thought nothing would help the guys in the workshop. "They are all hopeless and you can't teach them anything," he said. "They just don't care."

He also knew he couldn't carry on with things the way they were.

Greg came and had a talk with us, and everyone thought it would be a good thing to sign up. We agreed Greg should come and do an Alignment Report for us. This turned out to be very healthy, as it made us think about the future. In truth, I really pushed for it, as I knew Preben and Jakob needed to do things differently.

Anyway, we didn't sign up with *Action* right away, since it was just before Christmas and everyone was very busy, and probably a bit scared, to commit.

## The Moment of Truth

It all came to a head just days before Christmas. Preben had some really bad days with "the boys" and came to Jakob and said, "I've had enough. I can't take it anymore!"

My first thought was to call Greg and talk to him about what we could do to turn Preben around to being happy again.

That was when we signed up with *Action* and started our coaching program with Albert.

One of the first things Greg asked us to do was to read *The E-Myth Revisited,* which taught us how, in every business, there is a technician, an entrepreneur, and a manager. It showed us how the different types of people look at things differently.

We also found out who is who in our business. Jakob is the entrepreneur who looks to the future, Preben is the technician who looks at today, and I am the manager who looks at the past.

Greg then asked us what our weekly/monthly sales were. We really couldn't tell him. Any Key Performance Indicators that he asked for, we also couldn't supply.

It was a real awakening for us all. We then knew what we needed to do but had no idea how we would get the time to do it.

Greg suggested we produce a Procedures Manual.

As we didn't have a Mission Statement, Vision Statement, or Culture in place, or even an organizational chart, we clearly had a lot to do. It took us quite a while to get through some of the ideas and suggestions that Greg gave us. Slowly it all came together. Greg was very patient but kept pushing us forward. It got to the point where we really looked forward to the coaching calls. When we began to have the figures we needed, it was very easy to move forward. We also uncovered a lot of things that needed tightening.

## The Coach's Story

DK Design Kitchens was an unusual case for me, insofar as I was approached by one of the owners' wives (Pernille), and not the owner himself (Preben). This was out of utter frustration with her husband, whom she knew needed help, as business was overwhelming them.

To compound matters, the business was a partnership and it was not the dominant owner's wife who contacted me.

So both owners were *not* on board when coaching began.

The one owner (Preben) decided to give it a go, as nothing else was working. Jakob just said "OK" and went along with it. It was obvious from day one that both were not in alignment and Jakob was not on board.

I actually felt like walking away from this situation, however Pernille virtually begged me not to.

I then took a stand as a Coach and stepped up.

I demanded to call a four-hour manager's team meeting at which I would present. My attitude was that I would either "crash or burn" there. I spent time talking about the psychology of success in people and business. I was really talking to Jakob, hoping he would get it. It was very intense.

Well, he did. He called me two days later and said, "OK, I get it. I need to change. I am ready." The coaching was on course from that point on.

The situation was that the business was running, yet the major items like culture, the team, or going the extra mile were not happening. This is where I spent most of the early time—basically getting Jakob and Preben to become real leaders by inspiring people to follow, rather than just telling them what to do!

We spent time developing all the *spiritual* points of the business first—Culture, Vision, Mission, Rules, etc. We then relaunched the company as a Team.

Once this had taken place, we worked on the development of the sales team and the marketing activities. I must say, I cannot recall anything that really did not work, as by now Testing & Measuring was a culture embedded into the way things were done. We tried different techniques and methods until they worked.

One interesting thing was that we came up with a slogan "Dare to Be Different." We tried an advertisement that went against all advertising principles—it was a plain white rectangle with "Dare to Be Different" in the middle. The company's name, in very small lettering, was at the bottom. *That was all.* You can imagine how weird this looked among all the normal kitchen ads that contained offers and pictures. It worked! Not only did the leads increase, but we received a higher level of client. Their target market now was $15,000+ kitchens.

Once this was all working efficiently, we put Key Performance Indicators (KPIs) and management tools in place, and spent a long time on the financial management side of the business. Soon we had spreadsheets and graphs for everything from Cashflow and Sales, to Conversion and Factory Efficiency. This really gave them a sense of understanding and control of their business.

## The Outcome

By having systems and reporting KPIs in place, DK Design Kitchens now has a solid business, so much so that it is purchasing its own purpose-built facilities and moving out of rented premises to start the next growth phase.

"Our biggest achievement was working out the new price list, and changing the commission structure and quotation method," Pernille says. "We lost some sales staff and took on new ones, and we now have better profit than ever. Greg really has us focused on profit, not turnover. As a result, we were suddenly making more profit with a lot less effort."

Getting the rest of the team involved was the next challenge.

"We had Greg give the team members training and motivation to keep them focused, and we put KPIs in place for them too. We even had Greg relaunch the company at our Christmas function. He introduced our new Vision, Mission, Culture, and rules of the game to the rest of the team. We really started to get results with less headaches, and business was fun again."

Having fun at work is so important, yet not many people realize that.

"Our aim was to get rid of the 'bad fruit' among the team and to get new, more productive personnel. We did this by letting them deselect themselves from our new culture and rules. There are, of course, still procedures which haven't been written down, but the company is running a lot smoother than before we met Greg Albert."

People are, of course, an important dynamic in any business. They come and go, and that's only natural. But when this happens, many businesses aren't able to cope. That's why it's so important to have systems in place.

"Our top salesperson decided to start his own business," continues Pernille. "Before, this would have been a disaster. Now, with systems in place—a great recruitment process and a KPI management system—we were able to not only replace him, but to hire others to grow the business as well."

Preben still looks after production, but now has a foreman who checks, measures and makes cutting lists, and he has also hired his own installers who fit with the culture. Jakob is now running design and sales. He looks after and supports his sales team, and has focused on setting and managing the KPIs.

During the past 12 months, their average dollar sale increased by 40 percent and they increased their prices by 10 percent. This resulted in an increase in turnover of 30 percent, but more significantly their profitability is much healthier.

Whereas the business previously ran at a slight loss, DK Design Kitchens has just managed to record a net profit of $250,000. The company's turnover was $3 million.

Pernille is still running administration, but due to the rest of the company's running smoother, the accounts, cashflow, and profit and loss functions are now reviewed monthly. Team members know their targets.

Pernille reports that they now have a happy team and the climate at "work" is excellent. "It is fun going to work. We have weekly sales/administration team meetings and the factory has weekly "wifle" (What I Feel Like Expressing) sessions where team members get together to freely express their feelings. This has helped to weed out all the negative elements, and we now have a proactive team."

Weekly/monthly statistics and comparisons are produced and the Salesperson of the Month is rewarded at the end of every month. Targets are set and closely monitored.

"We now feel we are in control of the business, and not the other way round. There is always a smile on the faces of Preben and Jakob, and the 'lows' are becoming more and more rare. You can feel the buzz in the air, and this rubs off on our customers. We are now booked months in advance!"

Of course, the company still faces challenges, which they try to solve as they arise. The difference now is that all challenges are analyzed and understood so they don't occur again.

"But as everyone knows, in small business everything has its ups and downs. We just tackle the challenges in a different way than what we did before," continues Pernille. "We now look for solutions and how we can add a system of our own. Incredibly, we have just purchased our own new factory, office, and showroom and are going to set it all up for perfect production and workflow. In fact, we will set it up now with everything we learned from Greg and *Action.* We are all very exited about what we have achieved and what we have today. We look forward to the future, and thank the day we called Greg and asked for help that fateful Christmas, when we basically had had enough!"

Can you see how all the elements we have discussed come together and result in synergy?

Suddenly the business is a very different one than what it was before. And so is the end result.

Synergy is a combination of individual "things" that together produce an amazing result. What goes into producing synergy will vary depending on your individual situation, but as the above real-life example shows, it's a complex phenomenon. It involves a complex mix of emotional and physical factors that can be simple or involved. This doesn't mean it's difficult to implement—far from it. You can start by simply creating the right environment for your team members when they show up at work. You could also improve the way they are treated by recognizing and appreciating their individual contributions to the overall well being of the business.

Group training sessions build team synergy and are effective in upgrading the skills of individual members. People learn better in groups, as they usually have different levels of knowledge and social skills. Individuals usually learn more from a group question-and-answer session than from studying at home at their own pace. The dynamics of group sessions are very powerful. They also do wonders for team building as well.

One of the primary reasons for organizing skill-based training sessions is the positive affect it has on team morale. Getting people to work as a team to achieve difficult tasks is a great way to achieve bonding. These sessions can be physical or mental. For instance, training sessions at paintball combat courses, rock climbing venues, and obstacle courses are a great test of endurance and ingenuity. Alternatively, group activities like quiz evenings or game nights also work well.

Synergy is simply the end result of your team-building strategies. It's that magical something that occurs when your team suddenly clicks together.

It's that which differentiates an ordinary team from a dream team.

Here's a great real-life example of what I'm talking about. It involves the efforts of Glen Gregory, a gifted businessman who runs a Harvey Norman franchise, and his team of dedicated people. It also involves Graham Dunkley, one of my Business Coaches.

Once again, I am going to use Glen and Graham's very own words, as theirs is a truly inspirational story.

Glen was the franchisee of Harvey Norman Computer Store in Maitland, New South Wales. This store had been operating for some eight or nine years, with two previous owners and a change of location three years before Graham was taken on as coach.

The store is part of a Harvey Norman complex with Electrical and Furniture in the same building. They all share a common entrance.

Always a profitable outlet, it boasted the smallest selling area of all the Group's outlets. Space was at a premium. The staff were mostly untrained and had mediocre sales experience, gained only from a wide range of previous employers. Only a few had a strong background in computer-related fields.

None of them, and that includes Glen, had any concept of a consistent, scripted sales process, repeated follow-up, the high-level of service necessary to create Raving Fans with a long lifetime relationship, or of giving the store the "wow" factor.

Until they took on a Business Coach, that is.

## Glen's Story

Glen had a hard, competitive youth, which drove his High D personality style, a natural instinct for business, a good reputation in the Harvey Norman Group, and a burning desire to do what Gerry Harvey (the Group's founder) had done! But his teen years had been unkind, and he had few assets to help get him there.

"Having the opportunity to be a Harvey Norman Franchisee is like waking up to a dream every morning," said Glen. "Gerry Harvey asks you to take up a franchise, for which you get to build your own empire. All proprietors want to be Number One, yet we all want to work together and help each other to make Harvey Norman the number one retail company in Australia and the world."

## The Moment of Truth

Glen never really experienced a moment of truth—or something that told him he needed help. Far from it. He was a young gun who knew he was good and thought he knew it all.

"I was achieving very good results with my first two franchises, with little experience or qualification, but I wanted to be better. I wanted to be Number One. I knew I had to widen my vision and knowledge in order to understand retail better, so I could sell more and make more," said Glen.

"As luck would have it, one of my staff and his father were Business Coaches and to me this sounded like what I needed to improve myself, yet I was skeptical as to how much it would help. But I was committed to continually improving my store and myself."

Graham talked him into taking on coaching. However, he later confessed that he was extremely skeptical at first—he could not see what a professional pharmacist could know, or for that matter, teach him about information technology or computer sales!

So, almost as a favor, he reluctantly agreed to Graham's proposition. "Hell, what did I have to lose?" laughed Glen. "If this guy was any good at all, I might learn a few things and what would be the harm in that?"

Graham started talking about living above the line, about testing and measuring, and leadership, and he made Glen read books!

Glen hated reading! But he got down to it and read motivational books and watched videos. He read about the myths we all believe, about entrepreneurs, and about how we get into business, and why we often end up hating what we once loved doing. He learned why, when we run out of ideas, we just keep doing the same things, which makes us quietly go crazy. And he read books about success.

"Graham promised that I would be able to achieve greater results, but it would all be up to me. I had to put the hard work in, and Graham would give me the tools to grow the business."

Graham then talked him into putting his entire team through a one-day sales course. Needless to say this included him too! The penny had dropped. They realized they could do other things besides discounting!

The team came back all fired up.

Glen then had his coach put them through team training, and once again he included himself in that team. He suddenly realized that anyone can manage, but it takes skill to be a leader and to communicate well.

He began learning all about leverage in business.

Glen and his team were taught that all the national advertising in the world only gets the prospect to the door. What the team does from that moment on, to make it a memorable buying experience, is what explodes a business and takes it to the top.

They learned that treating their clients with honour, respect, warmth, and empathy creates a long-term trusting relationship, which then spawns greater opportunities for profitable sales than all the incessant giveaways that are traditionally featured in TV advertising.

Suddenly their conversion rate, transaction rate, and profitability climbed, and best of all, this great new team started having fun!

"Over the course of 12 months, with Graham as my mentor, I was able to learn the values of a team and how to use it to greater effect. I began to understand the business cycle where Boss looks after Staff, Staff look after Customers, Customers look after the Business, and the Business looks after the Boss. Simple, but solid," Glen continued.

"Watching *Action's* video seminars, reading some suggested books, studying direct-marketing methods, feeding and bouncing ideas off Graham—every week I was learning something new. I began looking at my business in a different way."

## Coach's Comment

Glen, always a good manager, quickly became one of the Harvey Norman Group's star franchisees, and his team came to be acknowledged as something special by the industry's account managers. Such was the store's performance that the national executive chose Glen to take on a fairly young and underperforming store in the northern suburbs of Perth.

So, eight months later, Glen and I parted company, the task at Maitland left unfinished. Maitland's loss was to be Perth's great gain—Glen's new store became one of the state's top three performers within 18 months.

Glen became so magnetic as a manager and leader that it wasn't long before three of the Maitland team joined him in Perth.

## The Outcome

From a reluctant, even cynical, beginning, Glen was hungry for new ideas and was able to apply them quickly. He conquered his shortcomings as a leader and communicator, rapidly gaining the wisdom to understand other personalities in his team and to get the best from them.

In only eight months, he grew his turnover by nearly 18 percent, from $9.2 million to over $11 million, and raised the profit from 10.1 percent to nearly 17 percent. His average unit sale climbed 16 percent to around $193. His annual client transaction rate rose by nearly 7 percent. And what's more, he achieved this during what is widely regarded as the poorest period in recent memory for computer sales across the nation, when many retailers were recording negative growth.

His team's efforts, spurred on by his infectious enthusiasm, made the Maitland store (which you might remember, had the smallest floor space of any Harvey Norman computer outlet) number three in profitability for the entire Group.

This is a great result by any standards. And even though Glen was working within a well-established franchise operation, having an independent, objective mentor paid off handsomely.

"As Harvey Norman franchisees, when we are looking at how to improve something within our business, we usually look at another Harvey Norman stores or even at our competition. With **ActionCOACH** being involved with thousands of companies, I found that working with Graham enabled me to draw on companies that were in different industries, yet had great ideas that could be applied to my store," explained Glen.

"Without doubt, my 12 months with Graham strengthened my ability to be the Number One Franchisee within Harvey Norman. My team at the Maitland store was exactly that—a *team*. The whole team wanted to be Number One. We all wanted to make a higher gross profit. We all wanted to sell more. We all wanted to provide the highest level of customer service possible. The whole team was involved in training and enjoyed the challenge of improving ourselves."

Even though Glen was a really good businessman before he took on a Coach, that didn't prevent him from reaching new levels of excellence.

"I was achieving good results before *Action International*, but I wasn't content with how much I really knew and wanted to step up a few levels. Today, I am a better Harvey Norman proprietor and a better businessman. I believe within Harvey Norman we all could be better businessmen."

# CONCLUSION

This book is all about your team members: those very special people who drive your business each and every day.

It's about real people who make a valuable contribution to your livelihood. It's about those without whom you simply wouldn't be where you are today.

I know it's one of the oldest clichés in business, but your team members really are one of your greatest assets. Do you treat them as such? Are they firing on all cylinders? Is your business feeling the full effects of their true potential?

Neglecting the team has got to be one of the tragedies of modern day business. Get this area of your business into shape and you'll reap the rewards—big time. Your business will become the envy of everyone. It's as simple as that.

Just look at the state of modern business and you'll soon realize that working on your team is one of the last untapped areas any businessperson can concentrate on that will work quick wonders for the bottom line in more ways than one. A recent Australian survey revealed that some 85 percent of all workers reported being bullied at work. That's shocking and disgraceful! Just think of the effects on productivity, shrinkage, motivation—in fact, on business in general.

After having worked your way through this book, you won't fall into the same trap that most businesspeople do when it comes to dealing with their people. You will have all the knowledge required to transform your team into your *dream team.* You will be able to make team members feel not only part of the family, but proud to be part of your organization. They might even begin to feel possessive about their jobs.

You'll know everything there is to know about putting together the dream team. You'll know precisely what it takes to get your work environment just right. You see, you'll know how the human brain functions and how to harness its true potential, not only for your benefit but also for that of your entire team. You'll begin to witness the workings of leverage in your business, perhaps for the very first time, as your team begins pulling together. You'll marvel at the power of synergistic teamwork, and wonder why you never strived to achieve this before.

By the time you reach the end of this book, you will be treating your people like real people. You'll have noticed that I never refer to mine as staff. I call them *my team.* We all have an important part to play and theirs is certainly in no way inferior to mine. For this reason I don't refer to them as a "human resource." They are not a resource. They are real human beings who deserve to be respected and treated fairly and with dignity.

I hope you have picked up on this thread that runs through this book.

Look after your team members and they will look after you.

# Getting into *Action*

## So, when is the best time to start?

*Now*—right now—so let me give you a step-by-step method to get yourself onto the same success path of many of my clients and the clients of my team at **ActionCOACH.**

Start testing and measuring now.

You'll want to ask your customers and prospects how they found out about you and your business. This will give you an idea of what's been working and what hasn't. You also want to concentrate on the five areas of the business chassis. Remember:

1. Number of Leads from each campaign.
2. Conversion Rate from each and every campaign.
3. Number of Transactions on average per year per customer.
4. Average Dollar Sale from each campaign.
5. Your Margins on each product or service.

The Number of Leads is easy; just take a measure for four weeks, average it out, and multiply by 50 working weeks of the year. Of course you'd ask each lead where they came from so you've got enough information to make advertising decisions.

The Conversion Rate is a little trickier, not because it's hard to measure, but because we want to know a few more details. You want to know what level of conversion you have from each and every type of marketing strategy you use. Remember that some customers won't buy right away, so keep accurate records on each and every lead.

To find the Number of Transactions you'll need to go through your records. Hopefully you can find the transaction history of at least 50 of your past customers and then average out their yearly purchases.

The Average Dollar Sale is as simple as it sounds. The total dollars sold divided by the number of sales. The best information you can collect is the average from each marketing campaign you run, so that you know where the real profit is coming from.

And, of course, your margins. An Average Margin is good to know and measure, but to know the margins on everything you sell is the most powerful knowledge you can collect.

If you're having any challenges with your testing and measuring, be sure to contact your nearest **ActionCOACH** Business Coach. She'll be able to help you through and show you the specialized documents to use.

If, by chance, you're thinking of racing ahead before you test and measure, remember this. It's impossible to improve a score when you don't know what the score is.

So you've got your starting point. You know exactly what's going on in your business right now. In fact, you know more about not only what's happening right now, but also the factors that are going to create what will happen tomorrow.

The next step in your business growth is simple.

Let's decide what you want out of the business—in other words, your goals. Here are the main points I want you to plan for.

How many hours do you want to work each week? How much money do you want to take out of the business each month? And, most importantly, when do you want to finish the business?

By "finish" the business, I mean when it will be systematized enough so it can run without your having to be there. Remember this about business; a little bit of planning goes a long way, but to make a plan you have to have a destination.

Once again, if you're having difficulty, talk to an **ActionCOACH** Business Coach. He'll know exactly how to help you find what it is you really want out of both your business and your life.

Now the real work begins.

Remember, our goal is to get a 10 percent increase in each area over the next 12 months. Choose well, but I want to warn you of one thing, one thing I can literally guarantee.

Eight out of 10 marketing campaigns you run *will not work.*

That's why when you choose to run, say, an advertising campaign in your local newspaper, you've got to run at least 10 different ads. When you select a direct mail campaign, you should send out at least 10 different letters to test, and so on.

Make sure you get at least five strategies under each heading and plan to run at least one, preferably two, at least each month for the next 12 months.

Don't work on just one of the five areas at a time; mix it up a little so you get the synergy of all five areas working together.

Now, this is the most important advice I can give you:

Learn how to make each and every strategy work. Don't just think you know what to do; go through my hints and tips, read more books, listen to as many tapes as you can, watch all the videos you can find, talk to the experts, and make sure you get the most advantage you can before you invest a whole lot of money.

The next 12 months are going to be a matter of doing the numbers, running the campaigns, testing headlines, testing offers, testing prices, and, of course, measuring the results.

By the end of it you should have at least five new strategies in each of the five areas working together to produce a great result.

Once again I want to stress that this will work and this will make your business grow as long as *you* work it.

Is it simple? *Yes.*

Is it easy? *No.*

You'll have to work hard. If you can get the guidance of someone who's been there before you, then get it.

Whatever you do, start it now, start it today, and most importantly, make the most of every day. Your past does not equal your future; you decide your future right here and right now.

*Be* who you want to be, *do* what you need to do, in order to *have* what you want to have.

Positive *thought* without positive *Action* leaves you with positively *nothing.* I called my company **ActionCOACH** for this very reason.

So take the first step—and get into *Action.*

# ABOUT THE AUTHOR

## Bradley J. Sugars

Brad Sugars is a world-renowned Australian entrepreneur, author, and business coach who has helped more than a million clients around the world find business and personal success.

He's a trained accountant, but as he puts it, most of his experience comes from owning his own companies. Brad's been in business for himself since age 15 in some way or another, although his father would argue he started at 7 when he was caught selling his Christmas presents to his brothers. He's owned and operated more than two dozen companies, from pizza to ladies fashion, from real estate to insurance and many more.

His main company, **ActionCOACH,** started from humble beginnings in the back bedroom of a suburban home in 1993 when Brad started teaching business owners how to grow their sales and marketing results. Now **ActionCOACH** has over 1000 franchises in 26 countries and is ranked in the top 100 franchises in the world.

Brad Sugars has spoken on stage with the likes of Tom Hopkins, Brian Tracy, John Maxwell, Robert Kiyosaki, and Allen Pease, written books with people like Anthony Robbins, Jim Rohn, and Mark Victor Hansen, appeared on countless TV and radio programs and in literally hundreds of print articles around the globe. He's been voted as one of the Most Admired Entrepreneurs by the readers of *E-Spy* magazine—next to the likes of Rupert Murdoch, Henry Ford, Richard Branson, and Anita Roddick.

Today, **ActionCOACH** has coaches across the globe and is ranked as one of the Top 25 Fastest Growing Franchises on the planet as well as the #1 Business Consulting Franchise. The success of **ActionCOACH** is simply attributed to the fact that they apply the strategies their coaches use with business owners.

Brad is a proud father and husband, the chairman of a major children's charity, and in his own words, "a very average golfer."

Check out Brad's Web site *www.bradsugars.com* and read the literally hundreds of testimonials from those who've gone before you.

# RECOMMENDED READING LIST

## ACTIONCOACH BOOK LIST

"The only difference between *you* now and *you* in 5 years' time will be the people you meet and the books you read." Charlie Tremendous Jones

"And, the only difference between *your* income now and *your* income in 5 years' time will be the people you meet, the books you read, the tapes you listen to, and then how *you* apply it all." Brad Sugars

- Brad Sugars "MindRICH" 3-hour Video
- Leverage—Board Game by Brad Sugars
- Action Speaks Louder than Words and 6 Steps to a Better Business CD or DVD. FREE OF CHARGE to Business Owners
- *The E-Myth Revisited* by Michael E. Gerber
- *My Life in Advertising & Scientific Advertising* by Claude Hopkins
- *Tested Advertising Methods* by John Caples
- *Building the Happiness Centered Business* by Dr. Paddi Lund
- *Write Language* by Paul Dunn & Alan Pease
- *7 Habits of Highly Effective People* by Steven Covey
- *First Things First* by Steven Covey
- *Awaken the Giant Within* by Anthony Robbins
- *Unlimited Power* by Anthony Robbins
- *22 Immutable Laws of Marketing* by Al Ries & Jack Trout
- *21 Ways to Increase Your Advertising Response* by Mark Tier
- *The One Minute Salesperson* by Spencer Johnson & Larry Wilson
- *The One Minute Manager* by Spencer Johnson & Kenneth Blanchard
- *The Great Sales Book* by Jack Collis
- *Way of the Peaceful Warrior* by Dan Millman

***To order Brad Sugars' products from the recommended reading list, call your nearest ActionCOACH office today.**

# The 18 Most Asked Questions about Working with an ActionCOACH Business Coach

## And 18 great reasons why you'll jump at the chance to get your business flying and make your dreams come true

### 1. So who is ActionCOACH?

**ActionCOACH** is a business Coaching and Consulting company started in 1993 by entrepreneur and author Brad Sugars. With offices around the globe and business coaches from Singapore to Sydney to San Francisco, **ActionCOACH** has been set up with you, the business owner, in mind.

Unlike traditional consulting firms, **ActionCOACH** is designed to give you both short-term assistance and long-term training through its affordable Mentoring approach. After 14 years teaching business owners how to succeed, **ActionCOACH**'s more than 10,000 clients and 1,000,000 seminar attendees will attest to the power of the programs.

Based on the sales, marketing, and business management systems created by Brad Sugars, your **ActionCOACH** is trained to not only show you how to increase your business revenues and profits, but also how to develop the business so that you as the owner work less and relax more.

**ActionCOACH** is a franchised company, so your local **ActionCOACH** is a fellow business owner who's invested her own time, money, and energy to make her business succeed. At **ActionCOACH,** your success truly does determine our success.

### 2. And, why do I need a Business Coach?

Every great sports star, business person, and superstar is surrounded by coaches and advisors.

And, as the world of business moves faster and gets more competitive, it's difficult to keep up with both the changes in your industry and the innovations in sales, marketing, and management strategies. Having a business coach is no longer a luxury; it's become a necessity.

On top of all that, it's impossible to get an objective answer from yourself. Don't get me wrong. You can survive in business without the help of a Coach, but it's almost impossible to thrive.

A Coach *can* see the forest for the trees. A Coach will make you focus on the game. A Coach will make you run more laps than you feel like. A Coach will tell it like it is. A Coach will give you small pointers. A Coach will listen. A Coach will be your marketing manager, your sales director, your training coordinator, your partner, your confidant, your mentor, your best friend, and an *Action* Business Coach will help you make your dreams come true.

**3. Then, what's an Alignment Consultation?**

Great question. It's where an *Action* Coach starts with every business owner. You'll invest a minimum of $1295, and during the initial 2 to 3 hours your Coach invests with you, he'll learn as much as he can about your business, your goals, your challenges, your sales, your marketing, your finances, and so much more.

All with three goals in mind: To know exactly where your business is now. To clarify your goals both in the business and personally. And thirdly, to get the crucial pieces of information he needs to create your businesses *Action* Plan for the next 12 months.

Not a traditional business or marketing plan mind you, but a step-by-step plan of *Action* that you'll work through as you continue with the Mentor Program.

**4. So, what, then, is the Mentor Program?**

Simply put, it's where your *Action* Coach will work with you for a full 12 months to make your goals a reality. From weekly coaching calls and goal-setting sessions, to creating marketing pieces together, you will develop new sales strategies and business systems so you can work less and learn all that you need to know about how to make your dreams come true.

You'll invest between $995 and $10,000 a month and your Coach will dedicate a minimum of 5 hours a month to working with you on your sales, marketing, team building, business development, and every step of the *Action* Plan you created from your Alignment Consultation.

Unlike most consultants, your *Action* Coach will do more than just show you what to do. She'll be with you when you need her most, as each idea takes shape, as each campaign is put into place, as you need the little pointers on making it happen, when you need someone to talk to, when you're faced with challenges and, most importantly, when you're just not sure what to do next. Your Coach will be there every step of the way.

**5. Why at least 12 months?**

If you've been in business for more than a few weeks, you've seen at least one or two so called "quick fixes."

Most Consultants seem to think they can solve all your problems in a few hours or a few days. At *Action* we believe that long-term success means not just scraping the surface and doing it for you. It means doing it with you, showing you how to do it, working alongside you, and creating the success together.

Over the 12 months, you'll work on different areas of your business, and month by month you'll not only see your goals become a reality, you'll gain both the confidence and the knowledge to make it happen again and again, even when your first 12 months of Coaching is over.

**6. How can you be sure this will work in my industry and in my business?**

Very simple. You see at *Action,* we're experts in the areas of sales, marketing, business development, business management, and team building just to name a few. With 328 different profit-building strategies, you'll soon see just how powerful these systems are.

*You,* on the other hand, are the expert in your business and together we can apply the *Action* systems to make your business fly.

Add to this the fact that within the *Action* Team at least one of our Coaches has either worked with, managed, worked in, or even owned a business that's the same or very similar to yours. Your *Action* Coach has the full resources of the entire *Action* team to call upon for every challenge you have. Imagine hundreds of experts ready to help you.

### 7. Won't this just mean more work?

Of course when you set the plan with your *Action* Coach, it'll all seem like a massive amount of work, but no one ever said attaining your goals would be easy.

In the first few months, it'll take some work to adjust, some work to get over the hump so to speak. The further you are into the program, the less and less work you'll have to do.

You will, however, be literally amazed at how focused you'll be and how much you'll get done. With focus, an *Action* Coach, and most importantly the *Action* Systems, you'll be achieving a whole lot more with the same or even less work.

### 8. How will I find the time?

Once again the first few months will be the toughest, not because of an extra amount of work, but because of the different work. In fact, your *Action* Coach will show you how to, on a day-to-day basis, get more work done with less effort.

In other words, after the first few months you'll find that you're not working more, just working differently. Then, depending on your goals from about month six onwards, you'll start to see the results of all your work, and if you choose to, you can start working less than ever before. Just remember, it's about changing what you do with your time, *not* putting in more time.

**9. How much will I need to invest?**

Nothing, if you look at it from the same perspective as we do. That's the difference between a cost and an investment. Everything you do with your *Action* Coach is a true investment in your future.

Not only will you create great results in your business, but you'll end up with both an entrepreneurial education second to none, and the knowledge that you can repeat your successes over and over again.

As mentioned, you'll need to invest at least $1295 up to $5000 for the Alignment Consultation and Training Day, and then between $995 and $10,000 a month for the next 12 months of coaching.

Your Coach may also suggest several books, tapes, and videos to assist in your training, and yes, they'll add to your investment as you go. Why? Because having an *Action* Coach is just like having a marketing manager, a sales team leader, a trainer, a recruitment specialist, and corporate consultant all for half the price of a secretary.

**10. Will it cost me extra to implement the strategies?**

Once again, give your *Action* Coach just half an hour and he'll show you how to turn your marketing into an investment that yields sales and profits rather than just running up your expenses.

In most cases we'll actually save you money when we find the areas that aren't working for you. But yes, I'm sure you'll need to spend some money to make some money.

Yet, when you follow our simple testing and measuring systems, you'll never risk more than a few dollars on each campaign, and when we find the ones that work, we make sure you keep profiting from them time and again.

Remember, when you go the accounting way of saving costs, you can only ever add a few percent to the bottom line.

Following Brad Sugars' formula, your *Action* Coach will show you that through sales, marketing, and income growth, your possible returns are exponential.

The sky's the limit, as they say.

## 11. Are there any guarantees?

To put it bluntly, no. Your *Action* Coach will never promise any specific results, nor will she guarantee that any of your goals will become a reality.

You see, we're your coach. You're still the player, and it's up to you to take the field. Your Coach will push you, cajole you, help you, be there for you, and even do some things with you, but you've still got to do the work.

Only *you* can ever be truly accountable for your own success and at *Action* we know this to be a fact. We guarantee to give you the best service we can, to answer your questions promptly, and with the best available information. And, last but not least your *Action* Coach is committed to making you successful whether you like it or not.

That's right, once we've set the goals and made the plan, we'll do whatever it takes to make sure you reach for that goal and strive with all your might to achieve all that you desire.

Of course we'll be sure to keep you as balanced in your life as we can. We'll make sure you never compromise either the long-term health and success of your company or yourself, and more importantly your personal set of values and what's important to you.

## 12. What results have other business owners seen?

Anything from previously working 60 hours a week down to working just 10—right through to increases in revenues of 100s and even 1000s of percent. Results speak for themselves. Be sure to keep reading for specific examples of real people, with real businesses, getting real results.

There are three reasons why this will work for you in your business. Firstly, your *Action* Coach will help you get 100 percent focused on your goals and the step-by-step processes to get you there. This focus alone is amazing in its effect on you and your business results.

Secondly, your coach will hold you accountable to get things done, not just for the day-to-day running of the business, but for the dynamic growth of the business. You're investing in your success and we're going to get you there.

Thirdly, your Coach is going to teach you one-on-one as many of *Action's* 328 profit-building strategies as you need. So whether your goal is to be making more money, or working fewer hours or both inside the next 12 months your goals can become a reality. Just ask any of the thousands of existing *Action* clients, or more specifically, check out the results of 19 of our most recent clients shown later in this section.

## 13. What areas will you coach me in?

There are five main areas your *Action* Coach will work on with you. Of course, how much of each depends on you, your business, and your goals.

Sales. The backbone of creating a superprofitable business, and one area we'll help you get spectacular results in.

Marketing and Advertising. If you want to get a sale, you've got to get a prospect. Over the next 12 months your *Action* Coach will teach you Brad Sugars' amazingly simple streetwise marketing—marketing that makes profits.

Team Building and Recruitment. You'll never *wish* for the right people again. You'll have motivated and passionate team members when your Coach shows you how.

Systems and Business Development. Stop the business from running you and start running your business. Your Coach will show you the secrets to having the business work, even when you're not there.

Customer Service. How to deliver consistently, make it easy to buy, and leave your customers feeling delighted with your service. Both referrals and repeat business are centered in the strategies your Coach will teach you.

## 14. Can you also train my people?

Yes. We believe that training your people is almost as important as coaching you.

Your investment starts at $1500 for your entire team, and you can decide between five very powerful in-house training programs. From "*Sales Made Simple*" for your face-to-face sales team to "*Phone Power*" for your entire team's telephone etiquette and sales ability. Then you can run the "*Raving Fans*" customer service training or the "*Total Team*" training. And finally, if you're too busy earning a living to make any real money, then you've just got to attend our "*Business Academy 101.*" It will make a huge impact on your finances, business, career, family, and lifestyle. You'll be amazed at how much involvement and excitement comes out of your team with each training program.

### 15. Can you write ads, letters, and marketing pieces for me?

Yes. Your *Action* Coach can do it for you, he can train you to do it yourself, or we can simply critique the marketing pieces you're using right now.

If you want us to do it for you, our one-time fees start at just $1195. You'll not only get one piece; we'll design several pieces for you to take to the market and see which one performs the best. Then, if it's a critique you're after, just $349 means we'll work through your entire piece and give you feedback on what to change, how to change it, and what else you should do. Last but not least, for between $15 and $795 we can recommend a variety of books, tapes, and most importantly, Brad Sugars' Instant Success series books that'll take you step-by-step through the how tos of creating your marketing pieces.

### 16. Why do you also recommend books, tapes, and videos?

Basically, to save you time and money. Take Brad Sugars' *Sales Rich* DVD or Video Series, for instance. In about 16 hours you'll learn more about business than you have in the last 12 years. It'll also mean your *Action* Coach works with you on the high-level implementation rather than the very basic teaching.

It's a very powerful way for you to speed up the coaching process and get phenomenal rather than just great results.

### 17. When is the best time to get started?

Yesterday. OK, seriously, right now, today, this minute, before you take another step, waste another dollar, lose another sale, work too many more hours, miss another family event, forget another special occasion.

Far too many business people wait and see. They think working harder will make it all better. Remember, what you know got you to where you are. To get to where you want to go, you've got to make some changes and most probably learn something new.

There's no time like the present to get started on your dreams and goals.

### 18. So how do we get started?

Well, you'd better get back in touch with your *Action* Coach. There's some very simple paperwork to sign, and then you're on your way.

You'll have to invest a few hours showing them everything about your business. Together you'll get a plan created and then the work starts. Remember, it may seem like a big job at the start, but with a Coach, you're sharing the load and together you'll achieve great things.

# Here's what others say about what happened after working with an *Action* business coach

**Paul and Rosemary Rose—Icontact Multimedia**

"Our *Action* coach showed us several ways to help market our product. We went on to triple our client base and simultaneously tripled our profits in just seven months. It was unbelievable! Last year was our best Christmas ever. We were really able to spoil ourselves!"

**S. Ford—Pride Kitchens**

"In 6 months, I've gone from working more than 60 hours per week in my business to less than 20, and my conversion rate's up from 19 percent to 62 percent. I've now got some life back!"

**Gary and Leanne Paper—Galea Timber Products**

"We achieved our goal for the 12 months within a 6-month period with a 100 percent increase in turnover and a good increase in margins. We have already recommended and will continue to recommend this program to others."

**Russell, Kevin, John, and Karen—Northern Lights Power and Distribution**

"Our profit margin has increased from 8 percent to 21 percent in the last 8 months. *Action* coaching focussed us on what are our most profitable markets."

**Ty Pedersen—De Vries Marketing Sydney**

"After just three months of coaching, my sales team's conversion rate has grown from an average of less than 12 percent to more than 23 percent and our profits have climbed by more than 30 percent."

**Hank Meerkerk and Hemi McGarvey—B.O.P. School of Welding**

"Last year we started off with a profit forecast, but as soon as we got *Action* involved we decided to double our forecast. We're already well over that forecast again by two-and-a-half times on turnover, and profits are even higher. Now we run a really profitable business."

**Stuart Birch—Education Personnel Limited**

"One direct mail letter added $40,000 to my bottom line, and working with *Action* has given me quality time to work on my business and spend time with my family."

**Mark West—Wests Pumping and Irrigation**

"In four months two simple strategies have increased our business more than 20 percent. We're so busy, we've had to delay expanding the business while we catch up!"

**Michael Griffiths—Gym Owner**

"I went from working 70 hours per week *in* the business to just 25 hours, with the rest of the time spent working *on* the business."

**Cheryl Standring—In Harmony Landscapes**

"We tried our own direct mail and only got a 1 percent response. With *Action* our response rate increased to 20 percent. It's definitely worth every dollar we've invested."

**Jason and Chris Houston—Empradoor Finishing**

"After 11 months of working with *Action,* we have increased our sales by 497 percent, and the team is working without our having to be there."

**Michael Avery—Coomera Pet Motels**

"I was skeptical at first, but I knew we needed major changes in our business. In 2 months, our extra profits were easily covering our investment and our predictions for the next 10 months are amazing."

**Garry Norris—North Tax & Accounting**

"As an accountant, my training enables me to help other business people make more money. It is therefore refreshing when someone else can help me do the same. I have a policy of only referring my clients to people who are professional, good at what they do, and who have personally given me great service. *Action* fits all three of these criteria, and I recommend *Action* to my business clients who want to grow and develop their businesses further."

**Lisa Davis and Steve Groves—Mt. Eden Motorcycles**

"With *Action* we increased our database from 800 to 1200 in 3 months. We consistently get about 20 new qualified people on our database each week for less than $10 per week."

**Christine Pryor—U-Name-It Embroidery**

"Sales for August this year have increased 352 percent. We're now targeting a different market and we're a lot more confident about what we're doing."

**Joseph Saitta and Michelle Fisher—Banyule Electrics**

"Working with *Action,* our inquiry rate has doubled. In four months our business has changed so much our customers love us. It's a better place for people to work and our margins are widening."

**Kevin and Alison Snook—Property Sales**

"In the 12 months previous to working with *Action,* we had sold one home in our subdivision. In the first eight months of working with *Action,* we sold six homes. The results speak for themselves."

**Wayne Manson—Hospital Supplies**

"When I first looked at the Mentoring Program it looked expensive, but from the inside looking out, its been the best money I have ever spent. Sales are up more than $3000 per month since I started, and the things I have learned and expect to learn will ensure that I will enjoy strong sustainable growth in the future."

# ActionCOACH Contact Details

**ActionCOACH Global Office**

5781 S. Fort Apache Road, Las Vegas, NV 89148

Ph: +1 (702) 795 3188

Fax: +1 (702) 795 3183

Free Call: (888) 483 2828

**ActionCOACH** Offices around the globe:

Australia | Brazil | Canada | China | Dominican Republic | England

France | Germany | Hong Kong | India | Indonesia | Ireland | Malaysia

Mexico | New Zealand | Nigeria | Phillippines | Portugal | Puerto Rico

Scotland | Singapore | S. Africa | Spain | Taiwan | USA | Wales

## Here's how you can profit from all of Brad's ideas with your local ActionCOACH Business Coach

Just like a sporting coach pushes an athlete to achieve optimum performance, provides them with support when they are exhausted, and teaches the athlete to execute plays that the competition does not anticipate.

A business coach will make you run more laps than you feel like. A business coach will show it like it is. And a business coach will listen.

The role of an **ActionCOACH** Business Coach is to show you how to improve your business through guidance, support, and encouragement. Your coach will help you with your sales, marketing, management, team building, and so much more. Just like a sporting coach, your **ActionCOACH** Business Coach will help you and your business perform at levels you never thought possible.

Whether you've been in business for a week or 20 years, it's the right time to meet with and see how you'll profit from an **ActionCOACH.**

As the owner of a business it's hard enough to keep pace with all the changes and innovations going on in your industry, let alone to find the time to devote to sales, marketing, systems, planning and team management, and then to run your business as well.

As the world of business moves faster and becomes more competitive, having a Business Coach is no longer a luxury; it has become a necessity. Based on the sales, marketing, and business management systems created by Brad Sugars, your **ActionCOACH** is trained to not only show you how to increase your business revenues and profits but also how to develop your business so that you, as the owner, can take back control. All with the aim of your working less and relaxing more. Making money is one thing; having the time to enjoy it is another.

Your **ActionCOACH** Business Coach will become your marketing manager, your sales director, your training coordinator, your confidant, your mentor. In short, your **ActionCOACH** will help you make your business dreams come true.

## ATTENTION BUSINESS OWNERS
## You can increase your profits now

Here's how you can have one of Brad's **ActionCOACH** Business Coaches guide you to success.

Like every successful sporting icon or team, a business needs a coach to help it achieve its full potential. In order to guarantee your business success, you can have one of Brad's team as your business coach. You will learn about how you can get amazing results with the help of the team at **ActionCOACH.**

The business coaches are ready to take you and your business on a journey that will reward you for the rest of your life. You see, we believe **Action** speaks louder than words.

Complete and post this card to your local **ActionCOACH** office to discover how our team can help you increase your income today!

**ActionCOACH**

**The World's Number-1 Business Coaching Firm**

Name ................................................................................................................................................

Position ................................................................................................................................................

Company ................................................................................................................................................

Address ................................................................................................................................................

................................................................................................................................................

Country ................................................................................................................................................

Phone ................................................................................................................................................

Fax ................................................................................................................................................

Email ................................................................................................................................................

Referred by ................................................................................................................................................

## How do I become an ActionCOACH Business Coach?

If you choose to invest your time and money in a great business and you're looking for a white-collar franchise opportunity to build yourself a lifestyle, an income, a way to take control of your life and, a way to get great personal satisfaction ...

**Then you've just found the world's best team!**

Now, it's about finding out if you've got what it takes to really enjoy and thrive in this amazing business opportunity.

**Here are the 4 things we look for in every ActionCOACH:**

**1. You've got to love succeeding**

We're looking for people who love success, who love getting out there and making things happen. People who enjoy mixing with other people, people who thrive on learning and growing, and people who want to charge an hourly rate most professionals only dream of.

**2. You've got to love being in charge of your own life**

When you're ready to take control, the key is to be in business for yourself, but not by yourself. **ActionCOACH**'s support, our training, our world leading systems, and the backup of a global team are all waiting to give you the best chance of being an amazing business success.

**3. You've got to love helping people**

Being a great Coach is all about helping yourself by helping others. The first time clients thank you for showing them step by step how to make more money and work less within their business, will be the day you realize just how great being an **ActionCOACH** Business Coach really is.

**4. You've got to love a great lifestyle**

Working from home, setting your own timetable, spending time with family and friends, knowing that the hard work you do is for your own company and, not having to climb a so-called corporate ladder. This is what lifestyle is all about. Remember, business is supposed to give you a life, not take it away.

Our business is booming and we're seriously looking for people ready to find out more about how becoming a member of the **ActionCOACH** Business Coaching team is going to be the best decision you've ever made.

**Apply online now at www.actioncoach.com**

## Here's how you can network, get new leads, build yourself an instant sales team, learn, grow and build a great team of supportive business owners around you by checking into your local ActionCOACH Profit Club

**Joining your local ActionCOACH Profit Club is about more than just networking, it's also the learning and exchanging of profitable ideas.**

Embark on a journey to a more profitable enterprise by meeting with fellow, like-minded business owners.

An **ActionCOACH** Profit Club is an excellent way to network with business people and business owners.You will meet every two weeks for breakfast to network and learn profitable strategies to grow your business.

Here are three reasons why **ActionCOACH** Profit Clubs work where other networking groups don't:

1. You know networking is a great idea. The challenge is finding the time and maintaining the motivation to keep it up and make it a part of your business. If you're not really having fun and getting the benefits, you'll find it gets easier to find excuses that stop you going. So, we guarantee you will always have fun and learn a lot from your bi-weekly group meetings.
2. The real problem is that so few people do any work 'on' their business. Instead they generally work "in" it, until it's too late. By being a member of an **ActionCOACH** Profit Club, you get to attend FREE business-building workshops run by Business Coaches that teach you how to work "on" your business and avoid this common pitfall and help you to grow your business.
3. Unlike other groups, we have marketing systems to assist in your groups' growth rather than just relying on you to bring in new members. This way you can concentrate on YOUR business rather than on ours.

Latest statistics show that the average person knows at least 200 other contacts. By being a member of your local **ActionCOACH** Profit Club, you have an instant network of around 3,000 people.

**Join your local ActionCOACH Profit Club today.**

**Apply online now at www.actionprofitclub.com**

## LEVERAGE—The Game of Business
## Your Business Success is just a Few Games Away

Leverage—The Game of Business is a fun way to learn how to succeed in business fast.

**The rewards start flowing the moment you start playing!**

Leverage is three hours of fun, learning, and discovering how you can be an amazingly successful business person.

It's a breakthrough in education that will have you racking up the profits in no time. The principles you take away from playing this game will set you up for a life of business success. It will open your mind to what's truly possible. Apply what you learn and **sit back and watch your profits soar.**

By playing this fun and interactive business game, you will learn:

- How to quickly raise your business income
- How business people can become rich and successful in a short space of time
- How to create a business that works without you

**Isn't it time you had the edge over your competition?**

Leverage has been played by all age groups from 12-85 and has been a huge learning experience for all. The most common comment we hear is: 'I thought I knew a lot, and just by playing a simple board game I have realized I have a long way to go. The knowledge I've gained from playing Leverage will make me thousands! Thanks for the lesson.'

**To order your copy online today, please visit** www.bradsugars.com

www.ingramcontent.com/pod-product-compliance
Lightning Source LLC
Chambersburg PA
CBHW060341100426
42812CB00003B/1082

*9780071831611*